Flavour

Flavour

Lwe Sabrina x

SABRINA GHAYOUR

ASTER*

For Connor and Olly . . .
. . . who have both taught me more about food and life than they'll ever know.
I'm so happy that you've become more adventurous eaters and I'm very proud
of you both. Here's to many, many adventures ahead!

ASTER*

First published in Great Britain in 2023
by Aster, an imprint of
Octopus Publishing Group Ltd
Carmelite House
50 Victoria Embankment
London EC4Y 0DZ
www.octopusbooks.co.uk

An Hachette UK Company
www.hachette.co.uk

ISBN 978 1 78325 510 8

A CIP catalogue record for this book is
available from the British Library.

Printed and bound in Italy

10 9 8 7 6 5 4 3 2 1

Publisher: Stephanie Jackson
Senior Managing Editor: Sybella Stephens
Copy Editor: Jo Richardson
Art Director: Jaz Bahra
Photographer: Kris Kirkham
Food Stylist: Laura Field
Props Stylist: Agathe Gits
Senior Production Manager: Peter Hunt

Author's notes
Sabrina uses level baking spoon measures,
unless specified otherwise.
Look for the V symbol on cheese and
wine vinegars to ensure they are suitable
for vegans.

Contents

Introduction

The more books I write, the more I learn about what truly matters versus what doesn't when cooking. One thing I have learned is that when all is said and done, no matter who we are, we all face very similar challenges at home when it comes to cooking: we are often time-poor and not always able to plan ahead, sometimes we don't have the right ingredients to hand, and more often these days, cost is an increasingly worrying factor.

Three words rule the recipes I like to write: simple, flavourful and economical . . . and in order to stick to these principles, I choose to write the kind of recipes that remain straight-forward, accessible, adaptable and always full of flavour.

Flavour is such an important element of my cooking. No matter what food I make, or where or what I eat, taste is everything. To me, flavour is comfort, satisfaction and even nostalgia, but importantly, it never has to be complicated, heavy-handed or extreme. Life is too short to eat bland food; sometimes a little seasoning, a flourish of herbs or a squeeze of lemon or drizzle of honey is all it takes to really elevate an otherwise simple dish into something that suddenly bursts with big, bold flavour. I get so much pleasure from the simplest of flavours that sometimes I wonder if all I need is salt and pepper to carry me through life. However, I have so much appreciation for a well-stocked kitchen cupboard, and for me, opening the door of my store cupboard can create a myriad of new possibilities, delivering endless combinations for vibrant and exciting new tastes using ingredients that you may also have tucked away in your cupboard.

By far the biggest lesson I have learned when it comes to cooking and writing recipes is that it takes a degree of bravery to keep things simple. Less is almost always more, and this is never a bad thing; in fact, almost a decade after my first book, *Persiana*, I can confirm that it is possibly one of the reasons my readers embrace my books and recipes as much as they do.

So, this book, lucky number 7, has been written to be full of flavour in the simplest and most pared-back way I know how. Many dishes are perfect for quick midweek meals, and others you may prefer to make when you have a little more time on your hands, but as always, you can easily chop and change ingredients if you need to, using up whatever you have at home or better suits your tastes. Have confidence to know that if an ingredient or method must be adhered to then I will always stress this in the recipe. So feel free to use these recipes as a great base for creating simple but vibrant meals in your own home. Nothing gives me greater joy than to hear when readers have embraced my recipes, and I love to learn about how dishes have evolved in different households when they have been made time and time again.

Whatever you like to eat and however much time and budget you have, there is plenty on offer for everyone in this book and almost everything can be adapted to suit every taste . . . so what are you waiting for? Dive in and explore this collection of colourful new recipes, that are, simply put, full of flavour!

Sabrina Ghayour

Salads

Aegean Giant Couscous Salad

For me, a salad has to pack in some big flavours, especially when using grains. I like mine to be savoury, sometimes sweet, sharp, refreshing, crunchy and aromatic, and for each mouthful to be a little well-seasoned flavour bomb that will make me want to eat more and more. The Turks have a word for recipes that have a slightly Aegean vibe – *ege* (pronounced eg-eh) – and if this wasn't my own creation, it would very much be an *ege salatasi*. This is sunshine and all its flavours packed into a salad; this is holidays in Turkey and Greece served on a plate . . . zingy, herby, crunchy and satisfying. I absolutely love this dish and serve it on repeat throughout the summer because it's a real crowd-pleaser.

SERVES 6–8

250g giant couscous

400g can chickpeas, drained

300g semi-dried tomatoes in oil, drained and cut into strips

250g block of halloumi cheese, grated

3 handfuls of pitted Kalamata olives

1 red pepper, cored, deseeded and finely diced

1 yellow or orange pepper, cored, deseeded and finely diced

1 red onion, finely chopped

50g pine nuts

1 small packet (about 30g) of dill, finely chopped

1 small packet (about 30g) of flat leaf parsley, finely chopped

1 small packet (about 30g) of mint, leaves finely chopped

finely grated zest and juice of 1 unwaxed lemon

olive oil

Maldon sea salt flakes and freshly ground black pepper

Cook the giant couscous according to the packet instructions, then drain, rinse thoroughly in cold water until completely cooled and leave to drain for a few minutes.

Tip the drained couscous into a mixing bowl, then add all the remaining ingredients, drizzle in some olive oil and season with a generous amount of salt and pepper. Mix really well until evenly combined, taste and adjust the seasoning if desired, then serve.

Serve with Dried Lime & Spice Marinated Lamb Chops (see page 95).

Beetroot & Pomegranate Salad

One of my favourite refrigerator staples is vacuum-packed beetroot, which I love for its versatility and long life. It's so flavoursome on its own that you really don't need many other ingredients to transform it into something wonderful. Its sweet nature pairs beautifully with fresh flavours and a little acidity, so the sharp taste of pomegranate molasses works perfectly with the beetroot, gently contrasted by refreshing sweet bursts of pomegranate seeds. This really is a beautiful salad and a perfect side for any meal.

SERVES 3–4

300g vacuum-packed cooked beetroot
  in natural juice, drained

100g pomegranate seeds

2 spring onions, thinly sliced
  diagonally from root to tip

½ small packet (about 15g) of dill,
  roughly chopped

2 tablespoons pomegranate molasses

1 tablespoon olive oil

1 teaspoon rice vinegar

Maldon sea salt flakes and freshly
  ground black pepper

Cut the beetroot into wedges or bite-sized chunks and put into a bowl.

Add all the remaining ingredients to the bowl and season with a generous amount of salt and pepper. Mix together well and serve.

Serve with Bean & Feta Patties (see page 82) or My Ultimate Mince & Aubergines (see page 100).

Chicken Shawarma Salad

We go through a lot of shawarma in my house, mainly because everyone loves kebabs. But when I'm feeling like I need a lighter meal, I make my chicken shawarma salad. It has all the components of a classic shawarma but with lettuce instead of flatbread and, truth be told, I love it. I also now bake the chicken in the oven so that it's even easier to make and means I can do other things around the house until it's ready. It is a wonderfully fresh, crunchy and satisfying salad, and should you have a bigger appetite, then yes of course, you can serve it with some wraps or flatbread on the side.

SERVES 4

For the chicken

600g boneless, skinless chicken thighs

4 tablespoons Greek-style yogurt, plus extra to serve

2 teaspoons garlic granules

2 teaspoons ground cumin

2 teaspoons ground coriander

2 teaspoons paprika

2 garlic cloves, crushed

juice of ½ lemon

1 tablespoon olive oil

Maldon sea salt flakes and freshly ground black pepper

For the salad

1 head of Romaine (Cos) lettuce, sliced

4 large tomatoes, halved and sliced

1 large red onion, halved and thinly sliced

4–6 large pickled cucumbers (the long Middle Eastern variety are ideal), sliced diagonally

½ small packet (about 15g) of fresh coriander, roughly chopped, plus extra to garnish (optional)

juice of ½ lemon

olive oil

chilli sauce, such as Sriracha, to serve

Preheat the oven to 210°C (190°C fan), Gas Mark 6½. Line a baking tray with baking paper.

Put all the chicken ingredients into a mixing bowl and season generously with salt and pepper, then use your hands to mix well and ensure the marinade coats the top and underside of each thigh.

Transfer the chicken thighs to the lined tray and roast for 40–45 minutes until lovely and charred and cooked through. Remove from the oven, slice the cooked chicken thinly and set aside.

Place all the salad ingredients together on a large platter. Squeeze over the lemon juice, add a little drizzle of olive oil and season well with salt and pepper, then gently toss together. Add the chicken slices and toss again, then drizzle with yogurt and some chilli sauce, and scatter over a little extra coriander if desired. This needs no accompaniment.

Cauliflower & Lentil Salad

I love lentils, especially in salads. Paired here with cauliflower and some sweet and spicy ingredients, this is one of those salads you won't be able to put down. Perfect on its own or with fish, chicken or pan-fried halloumi.

SERVES 6–8

250g uncooked green lentils

1 large cauliflower, broken into florets

olive oil

1 teaspoon paprika

1 teaspoon ground coriander

1 teaspoon ground cumin

1 teaspoon garlic granules

100g flaked almonds

250g dates, pitted, halved, thinly sliced into strips and then chopped

2 long red chillies, deseeded and finely chopped

1 small packet (about 30g) of flat leaf parsley, finely chopped

1 small packet (about 30g) of fresh coriander, finely chopped

Maldon sea salt flakes and freshly ground black pepper

For the dressing

4 tablespoons date molasses

3 tablespoons vegan red wine vinegar

2 tablespoons olive oil

Cook the lentils according to the packet instructions, then drain, rinse thoroughly in cold water, drain again and set aside.

Preheat the oven to 180°C (160°C fan), Gas Mark 4. Line a large baking tray with baking paper.

Place the cauliflower florets on the lined tray and drizzle generously with olive oil. Mix the spices and garlic granules together with a generous amount of salt and pepper and sprinkle over the florets, then use your hands to evenly coat them in the oil and spice mixture. Spread out in a single layer and roast for 30 minutes, adding the flaked almonds to the tray for the last 10 minutes of the cooking time. Remove from the oven.

Mix the dressing ingredients together with a generous seasoning of salt and pepper in a jug or small bowl.

Put the lentils into a mixing bowl, add a little olive oil and salt and pepper and mix together. Then add the dates, toasted flaked almonds, chillies, herbs and dressing and mix everything together well. Decant on to a large serving platter, top with the roasted cauliflower florets and serve.

Serve with Burnt Courgettes with Lemon & Feta Yogurt (see page 145).

Halloumi, Blood Orange & Pistachio Rocket Salad,

Halloumi makes any dish extra special, but this particular combination really works well with salty, sweet, crunchy and peppery components that deliver big on flavour and take no time to throw together. If you can't find blood oranges, ordinary oranges will absolutely do.

SERVES 2–4

2 blood oranges

250g block of halloumi cheese

olive oil

50g rocket leaves

½ red onion, halved and thinly sliced into half moons

30g pistachio slivers (or very roughly chopped whole nuts)

For the dressing

juice reserved from preparing the blood oranges

2 tablespoons vegan red wine vinegar

1 tablespoon olive oil

2 teaspoons marmalade

Maldon sea salt flakes and freshly ground black pepper

Using a sharp knife, cut a disc of peel off the top and base of each orange, then working from the top of the fruit downwards, cut away the remaining peel and pith in strips, just enough to expose the orange flesh, until the entire orange is peeled. Cut each orange in half widthways, then slice each half into half moons. Reserve any juice that is released from the oranges for the dressing.

Cut the halloumi into 7 slices and then cut each slice lengthways into 2 fingers. Place a frying pan over a medium-high heat, drizzle in some olive oil, and once hot, fry the halloumi fingers for a couple of minutes on each side until they are soft but deeply golden brown. Remove from the heat.

Arrange the rocket leaves on a large plate and add the fried halloumi and orange slices, then scatter with the red onion and pistachios. Mix the dressing ingredients together in a jug or small bowl, season well with salt and pepper and mix again, then pour over the salad. Serve immediately.

Serve with Bean, Pepper & Thyme Khorak (see page 141).

My Platter of Dreams

This collection of wonderful things that Persians, Arabs and Turks like to graze on really is everything I could hope to have served to me for a casual lunch with friends. All the elements are merely suggestions, but they certainly go well together and you can increase or decrease the offering and add your own twists very easily, exactly as you please. Get creative – and enjoy!

SERVES 4–6

3 medium eggs

150g baby plum tomatoes, halved

½ large cucumber, diced

½ red onion, diced

olive oil

1 teaspoon dried wild oregano, plus
    extra for sprinkling

1 teaspoon pul biber chilli flakes, plus
    extra for sprinkling

400g can chickpeas, drained

2 teaspoons za'atar, plus extra to serve

juice of ½ lemon

½ packet (about 15g) of fresh
    coriander, finely chopped

250g thick Greek yogurt

200g feta cheese, broken
    into 10–12 large chunks

handful of pitted Kalamata olives

handful of pitted green olives

Maldon sea salt flakes and freshly
    ground black pepper

bread, to serve (optional)

Cook the eggs in a small saucepan of boiling water for 7 minutes or so, then drain and cool under cold running water. Once cooled, shell, halve and set aside.

Put the tomatoes, cucumber and onion into a mixing bowl, add some salt and pepper, a light drizzle of olive oil, the oregano and pul biber and mix together.

In another bowl, mix the chickpeas with the za'atar, lemon juice, a light drizzle of olive oil, salt and pepper and the coriander.

Choose the largest platter you can find. Spoon the yogurt into a small bowl or into a corner of the platter. Arrange the tomato mixture, chickpeas, egg halves, feta and olives on the platter, drizzle the yogurt and feta with a little extra olive oil and sprinkle some extra oregano and pul biber wherever you like. In another small bowl, add extra za'atar mixed with a little olive oil for drizzling, and serve with bread, if desired.

Serve with Mama Ghanoush (see page 158).

'Hummus' Salad

I have written many a hummus recipe in my time, but I confess, I don't like to deviate too far from the original recipe because it's so wonderful in its simplicity. Having said that, one day when my food processor died on me and the prospect of hand-mashing chickpeas did not appeal, this happened . . . and that, dear friends, is what you call 'a happy accident'. All the joys and key ingredients of hummus with a few little twists, served as a salad so good in its own right that I wouldn't hesitate to serve hummus alongside it.

SERVES 2–4

400g can chickpeas, drained

2 preserved lemons, deseeded and
    finely chopped

½ small packet (about 15g) of flat leaf
    parsley, leaves picked

olive oil, for frying

4 garlic cloves, thinly sliced

For the dressing

3 tablespoons tahini

1 teaspoon garlic granules

juice of ½ lemon

3 tablespoons warm water

Maldon sea salt flakes and freshly
    ground black pepper

Mix the chickpeas, preserved lemons and parsley leaves together in a small bowl, then decant on to a serving platter.

Heat a small saucepan or frying pan over a medium heat and pour in about 1cm olive oil. Line a plate with a double layer of kitchen paper. Once the oil is hot, add the garlic slices and swirl them around until they are nicely golden brown all over, ensuring they do not burn (if they are browning too quickly, lift the pan off the heat and swirl the pan around). Remove with a slotted spoon and transfer to the paper-lined plate to drain.

Mix the dressing ingredients, except the warm water, together in a small bowl and season very generously with salt and pepper. Once combined, slowly mix in the water until the dressing reaches a pouring consistency.

Pour the dressing over the chickpeas. Top with the crispy garlic slices, season with pepper and serve.

Serve with Fatayer Puffs (see page 57).

Nectarine, Halloumi & Cucumber Salad with Cashews

I just love this salad. Sweet, citrusy, salty and crunchy, and with so much flavour packed into it that every mouthful is a different combination of happiness. It's easy to pull together and so colourful and pretty when on the plate. Best of all? It really doesn't involve much work. Perfect alongside any feast or as a lovely refreshing meal on its own.

SERVES 4

250g block of halloumi cheese

2 ripe nectarines

½ large cucumber

generous handful of cashew nuts

2 springs onions, thinly sliced diagonally from root to tip

olive oil

½ small packet (about 15g) of mint, leaves picked, rolled up tightly and thinly sliced into ribbons

½ small packet (about 15g) of dill, roughly chopped

½ teaspoon nigella seeds

½ teaspoon pul biber chilli flakes

juice of ½ orange

freshly ground black pepper

Cut the block of halloumi in half lengthways and cut each half into cubes.

Cut each nectarine in half, remove the stone and cut into 8 pieces.

Peel the cucumber, cut in half lengthways and scoop the seeds out with a teaspoon, then cut into 5mm-thick half moon slices.

Arrange the nectarines, cucumber, cashews and spring onions on a large platter.

Heat a frying pan over a medium-high heat, drizzle in a little olive oil and fry the halloumi for a couple of minutes on each side until nicely browned.

Arrange the fried halloumi in between the other ingredients on the platter and scatter over the herbs, nigella seeds and pul biber. Season with pepper, drizzle with olive oil and squeeze over the orange juice, then serve.

Serve with Cabbage 'Bowl' Dolma (see page 147).

Pistachio Pasta Salad with, Tomatoes, Olives & Red Onion

I have been making this salad for many years now using both the pistachio pesto with the recipe or – when I'm short of time and ingredients – shop-bought fresh basil pesto. We all make compromises sometimes, but I must admit I prefer the punchy combination of herbs in this pistachio pesto mix, brightened up even more with semi-roasted (aka sunblush or sun-dried) tomatoes and my favourite Kalamata olives and red onion. It's a lunchbox classic for me, and something I make in big quantities for the household to snack on over a few days. I also love serving it with roast chicken and as a picnic dish, too.

SERVES 4–6

250g of your favourite pasta shape

75g Parmesan cheese, roughly chopped

75g pistachio slivers (or very roughly chopped whole nuts)

2 garlic cloves, peeled

1 small packet (about 30g) of dill

1 small packet (about 30g) of fresh coriander

1 small packet (about 30g) of flat leaf parsley

juice of ½ fat lemon

300g semi-dried tomatoes in oil, drained and oil reserved, then cut widthways into strips

olive oil (optional)

1 red onion, halved and thinly sliced into half moons

2–3 generous handfuls of pitted Kalamata olives

Maldon sea salt flakes and freshly ground black pepper

Cook the pasta in a large saucepan of salted boiling water according to the packet instructions, then drain, rinse very well in cold water until completely cooled and leave to drain.

Put the Parmesan, pistachios, garlic and some salt and pepper into a small food processor and blitz together. Then add the herbs, lemon juice and the oil from the tomatoes and blitz until well combined. Add more olive oil as needed to enable the pesto to spin without making it too oily.

Add the drained pasta to a mixing bowl along with the tomatoes, onion and finally the pesto. Mix everything together, then stir in the olives. Taste and adjust the seasoning if desired. This needs no accompaniment.

Sweet & Fragrant Mushroom Salad

What may sound like a bizarre offering is actually so delicious that when I first created the recipe, I made it three days in a row. The flavours are inspired by Thailand, and the wonderful addition of toasted dry rice is a genius way of injecting a nutty, smoky flavour into the dish. This is great paired with some steamed rice.

SERVES 4–6

2 tablespoons uncooked basmati rice

600g chestnut mushrooms, quartered

4 spring onions, thinly sliced diagonally from root to tip

olive oil, for drizzling

½ red onion, halved and very thinly sliced into half moons

1 long red chilli, deseeded and very finely chopped

½ small packet (about 15g) of fresh coriander, roughly chopped

½ small packet (about 15g) of mint, leaves roughly chopped

For the dressing

finely grated zest and juice of 1 fat unwaxed lime

1 large garlic clove, minced

2 tablespoons caster sugar

1 tablespoon soy sauce

1 teaspoon sesame oil

freshly ground black pepper

Heat a dry frying pan over a medium-high heat, add the rice and toast, shaking the pan occasionally, for 2 minutes, or until the rice is deep golden brown all over, but not burnt. Remove from the heat and leave to cool.

Heat a large frying pan over a high heat, and once hot, add the mushrooms to the dry pan, allow them to release their liquid and then cook until the liquid has evaporated, stirring occasionally. Add a drizzle of olive oil to the pan and cook the mushrooms until browned. Remove from the heat and set aside.

Using a pestle and mortar, grind the toasted rice as finely as you can until you reach the consistency of coarse sand grains. Don't be tempted to use a spice or coffee grinder, as it will produce way too fine a powder.

Mix the dressing ingredients together in a small bowl until evenly combined.

Transfer the mushrooms to a mixing bowl and add the ground rice followed by the dressing and mix together really well. Add the spring onions, red onion, chilli and fresh herbs and mix again, then serve.

Serve with Roasted Vegetable & Mixed Bean Salad with Herb Dressing (see page 33).

Spice-roasted Butternut & Black Rice Salad

Big salads are among some of my favourite recipes to make. I'm not talking about limp, overdressed lettuce leaves – I mean substantial, flavourful combinations. Butternut squash has a natural sweetness and means you can throw so many bold flavours and spices at it and it just balances them out beautifully.

SERVES 6–8

1kg butternut squash, peeled, halved, deseeded and cut into 1.5cm slices

olive oil

1 teaspoon ground cumin

1 teaspoon ground cinnamon

1 teaspoon paprika

250g black rice

1 large red onion, finely chopped

100g dried cranberries

50g flaked almonds

250g pomegranate seeds

1 small packet (about 30g) of flat leaf parsley, leaves finely chopped

Maldon sea salt flakes and freshly ground black pepper

For the dressing

3 tablespoons pomegranate molasses

3 tablespoons olive oil

2 tablespoons honey or maple syrup

1 tablespoon vegan red wine vinegar

1 teaspoon ground cinnamon

Preheat the oven to 220°C (200°C fan), Gas Mark 7. Line a large baking tray with baking paper.

Place the butternut pieces on the lined tray and drizzle generously with olive oil. Mix the spices together and sprinkle over the pieces, then use your hands to evenly coat them in the oil and spice mix. Spread out in a single layer, season with salt and pepper and roast for 40 minutes or until starting to brown on the edges. Remove from the oven and leave to cool.

Cook the rice according to the packet instructions, then rinse in cold water until cooled, then drain and set aside.

Mix the onion, cranberries, flaked almonds, pomegranate seeds and parsley (reserving a little for garnish) in a bowl, then add the rice. Mix the dressing ingredients together, pour over the salad and stir in. Season generously with salt and pepper, mix again and leave to rest for 15 minutes. Stir again, taste and adjust the seasoning if desired, and serve with the roasted butternut arranged on top and scattered with the reserved parsley.

Serve with Ras el Hanout Sticky Spatchcock Poussin (see page 118).

Roasted Vegetable & Mixed Bean Salad with Herb Dressing

This is a great way to pack vegetables into a salad, but in the laziest one-tray bake kind of way! It is a lovely colourful dish to serve on its own or as part of a bigger feast. You can easily bulk the dish up by adding a grain of your choice, like brown or wild rice or barley, if you're feeding a crowd.

SERVES 3–4

1 large courgette, cut into 1cm-thick slices

1 large aubergine, peeled and cut into about 2cm chunks

1 large red pepper, deseeded and cut lengthways into 1cm-thick strips

olive oil

1 small red onion, finely chopped

400g can black beans, drained and rinsed

400g can cannellini beans, drained and rinsed

For the herb dressing

good squeeze of lemon juice

½ small packet (about 15g) of parsley

½ small packet (about 15g) of fresh coriander

2 garlic cloves

¼ teaspoon chilli flakes

1 tablespoon vegan red wine vinegar

1 heaped teaspoon caster sugar

Maldon sea salt flakes and freshly ground black pepper

Preheat the oven to 220°C (200°C fan), Gas Mark 7. Line your largest baking tray with baking paper.

Place the courgette, aubergine and red pepper on the tray, drizzle with olive oil and use your hands to coat the vegetables in oil, adding a little more if needed. Spread out in a single layer and roast for 30–35 minutes or until the vegetables are cooked through. Remove from the oven and leave to cool.

Add all the dressing ingredients, plus 5–6 tablespoons olive oil, to a bullet blender or food processor. Blitz until smooth, ensuring the garlic has blended. Taste and adjust the seasoning if desired.

Tip the cooked vegetables into a mixing bowl and add the chopped onion, and the drained black beans and cannellini beans. Pour over the dressing, mix well, then taste and adjust the seasoning if desired before serving.

Serve with Butterflied Lamb with Tahini Garlic Yogurt (see page 123).

Tuna, Tomato &
Borlotti Bean Salad,

I could quite simply enjoy the combination of tuna and beans with nothing more than some onion, salt, pepper and olive oil. But this salad is a riot of flavour that you will return to again and again. Leftovers make great packed lunches the next day, when the flavours will have intensified even more.

SERVES 6–8

3 x 145g cans tuna in oil, drained

2 x 400g cans borlotti beans, drained and rinsed

1 large red onion, finely chopped

1 small packet (about 30g) of flat leaf parsley, finely chopped

265g semi-dried tomatoes in oil, drained and oil reserved, then roughly chopped

250g baby plum tomatoes, sliced into thirds

juice of ½ lemon

1 heaped teaspoon garlic granules

1 heaped teaspoon pul biber chilli flakes

Maldon sea salt flakes and freshly ground black pepper

Put all the ingredients, except the oil from the tomatoes, into a mixing bowl and season generously with salt and pepper.

Pour over 2–3 tablespoons of the tomato oil, mix well and serve. This needs no accompaniment.

Spicy Beef, Cucumber & Herb Salad

I do love my seared beef salads, and I have made quite a few variations over the years simply because they are something I eat a lot of at home. Beef is very much the favourite, but you could use lamb or pork steaks, so go with whichever you prefer because the flavour combinations here are bold, refreshing and really pleasing.

SERVES 2

olive oil

300g sirloin or rump steak, cut into 1.5cm cubes

generous handful of fresh coriander

generous handful of basil leaves

generous handful of dill

½ red onion, halved and thinly sliced into half moons

½ large cucumber, peeled, halved lengthways and deseeded, then cut into 5mm-thick slices

50g pomegranate seeds

Maldon sea salt flakes and freshly ground black pepper

For the dressing

1 long red chilli, deseeded (or not if you prefer) and very finely chopped

1 fat garlic clove

finely grated zest and juice of 1 fat unwaxed lime

2 tablespoons olive oil

1 heaped teaspoon coriander seeds

1 tablespoon clear honey

Heat a frying pan over a high heat. Drizzle a little olive oil on to the steak pieces and rub in to coat them all over in the oil, then season well with pepper. Once the pan is hot, add the steak pieces to the pan and season with salt. Without stirring, let the steak pieces cook lightly for just under a minute on each side. Shake the pan vigorously, then remove from the heat.

Put all the dressing ingredients, except for the honey, and some salt and pepper into a bullet blender or mini food processor and blitz until smooth. Then add the honey and mix until evenly combined.

Roughly chop all the herbs and add them to a mixing bowl along with the steak pieces, red onion, cucumber, pomegranate seeds and dressing and toss together well, then serve. This needs no accompaniment.

Curried Potato Salad

I'm fairly sure I have made over a dozen different versions of potato salad over the years to appease my mother and her love for it, but this is altogether quite different and a nice change from the classic version. Curried anything is generally enough to lure me to eat something, but potatoes and curry spice are a great match. The crème fraîche is a great swap for mayonnaise as it's creamier, but somehow feels lighter and has a gentle acidity that works well with the potatoes, too.

SERVES 6–8

750g baby new potatoes

1 bunch of spring onions, thinly sliced
    from root to tip

300g crème fraîche

2 garlic cloves, crushed

2 green chillies, deseeded, very finely chopped

1 tablespoon caster sugar

1 heaped tablespoon medium curry powder

1 small packet (about 30g) of fresh coriander,
    finely chopped (reserve a handful for
    garnish)

2 tablespoons olive oil

Maldon sea salt flakes and freshly ground
    black pepper

Cook the potatoes whole in a saucepan of boiling water for about 15 minutes until cooked through and tender. Drain and rinse in cold water until cool. Roughly chop the potatoes.

Put the potatoes into a mixing bowl, then add all the remaining ingredients and a generous amount of salt and pepper. Mix everything together really well and serve scattered with chopped coriander.

Serve with My Tender TFC (see page 99) or Pan-fried Salmon with Barberry Butter (see page 133).

'Warm Harissa Broccoli & Black Rice Salad,

I love using black rice in recipes because, whatever you add to it, it provides a beautiful contrast to the colours of the other ingredients, not to mention its pleasingly nutty and chewy texture. This is a quick throw-together using ingredients I keep handy at home. The result is fantastic: sweet, crunchy, spicy and just a little zingy, too. It's definitely one to remember when you want a simple yet delicious accompaniment to your meal.

SERVES 3–4

150g black rice

200g Tenderstem broccoli

200g semi-dried tomatoes in oil, drained (reserve the oil), then cut into strips

1 tablespoon rose harissa

finely grated zest and juice of 1 unwaxed lemon

1 heaped tablespoon clear honey (if vegan, use maple syrup)

Maldon sea salt flakes and freshly ground black pepper

Cook the rice according to the packet instructions.

Meanwhile, bring a saucepan of water to the boil, add the Tenderstem broccoli and cook for 6 minutes. Drain, cut into bite-sized pieces and put into a mixing bowl.

Add the tomatoes and 2–3 tablespoons of the reserved oil to the bowl and mix well. Then add the harissa and lemon zest and juice, and season generously with salt and pepper.

Once the rice is cooked, drain if necessary and add it to the broccoli and tomato mixture. Add the honey (or maple syrup), mix together well and serve.

Serve with Smoked Aubergine with Lime & Maple Dressing (see page 142).

Warm Orzo, Black-eyed Bean, & Herb Salad

I love pasta and I love pulses, and this recipe combines them beautifully with the addition of an abundance of fragrant herbs, which elevates the dish to another level. I'm not really sure if it's a salad or a warm bean dish, but it is definitely something I don't want to stop dipping my spoon into before serving. It really is that delicious.

SERVES 4–6

250g orzo pasta

olive oil

2 garlic cloves, crushed

3 tablespoons tomato purée

400g can black-eyed beans, drained and rinsed

1 small packet (about 30g) of flat leaf parsley, finely chopped

1 small packet (about 30g) of dill, finely chopped

1 small packet (about 30g) of fresh coriander, finely chopped

1 small packet (about 30g) of chives, thinly sliced

juice of ½ lemon

Maldon sea salt flakes and freshly ground black pepper

Cook the orzo in a large saucepan of salted boiling water according to the packet instructions, then drain and return to the pan, but turn the heat off.

Drizzle generously with olive oil and add the garlic and tomato purée, then work into the orzo until evenly combined. Season well with salt and pepper and add the beans, chopped herbs and lemon juice and mix well. Taste and adjust the seasoning if desired, then serve.

Serve with Charred Broccoli with Lemons, Chillies & Yogurt (see page 154).

Watermelon, Chicory & Ricotta Salad

By now you must know that I adore fresh fruit in salads, and watermelon feels especially right to me because Persians (and indeed Turks, Greeks and Arabs) love it so much. This is perhaps a little unorthodox as a combination, but the sweet watermelon, slightly bitter chicory and creamy ricotta work so well with the dressing to ensure that every bite is juicy and refreshing, with a lovely creaminess on the finish from the ricotta. It's simple, colourful and flavourful – my three favourite characteristics combined.

SERVES 4–6

2 heads of red and green chicory, leaves separated

350g watermelon flesh, cut into 2.5cm cubes

250g ricotta cheese

75g walnuts

1 teaspoon pul biber chilli flakes

handful of mint, leaves picked, rolled up tightly and thinly sliced into ribbons

For the dressing

finely grated zest and juice of 1 fat unwaxed lime

2 tablespoons clear honey

1 tablespoon olive oil

Maldon sea salt flakes and freshly ground black pepper

Arrange the chicory leaves and watermelon on a large platter. Dot with dollops of the ricotta all over and scatter over the walnuts.

Mix the dressing ingredients together with a generous seasoning of salt and pepper in a jug or small bowl, then pour over the salad.

Sprinkle with the pul biber and finish with the mint, then serve.

Serve with Ras el Hanout Sticky Spatchcock Poussin (see page 118).

Tamarind Prawn Vermicelli with Orange & Pomegranate & Herbs

This refreshing noodle salad has bags of flavour in every bite. You might think it strange to combine oranges and pomegranates with prawns, but you'd be wrong – those little bursts of sweetness work perfectly with the sharpness of the dressing, and the fresh herbs make the whole dish look like a work of art.

SERVES 2–4

100g rice vermicelli

1 orange

150g cooked peeled tiger prawns

½ red onion, halved and thinly sliced into half moons

4 spring onions, thinly sliced from root to tip

100g pomegranate seeds

½ small packet (about 15g) of fresh coriander, finely chopped

½ small packet (about 15g) of mint, leaves picked, rolled up tightly and thinly sliced into ribbons

For the dressing

2 tablespoons olive oil

1 tablespoon tamarind paste

2 tablespoons caster sugar

1 fat garlic clove, minced

1 teaspoon pul biber chilli flakes

Maldon sea salt flakes and freshly ground black pepper

Cook the vermicelli according to the packet instructions, then drain, plunge into cold water until completely cooled and drain again. Set aside.

Using a sharp knife, cut a disc of peel off the top and base of the orange, then working from the top of the fruit downwards, cut away the remaining peel and pith in strips, just enough to expose the orange flesh, until the entire orange is peeled. Cut the orange in half widthways, then cut each half into half moons.

Mix the dressing ingredients together in a large mixing bowl until well combined.

Add the vermicelli, oranges and the remaining ingredients to the bowl containing the dressing and mix everything together. Taste and adjust the seasoning if desired, then serve. This needs no accompaniment.

Light Bites & Savoury Treats

Carrot, Oregano & Feta Börek Swirls

Börek are versatile enough to accommodate a variety of different fillings; classic fillings are usually minced lamb, cheese or spinach, but this carrot, oregano and feta börek is not only delicious but also really quite beautiful and, I'm pleased to say, really quite easy to make.

MAKES 6

1kg carrots, peeled and chopped into 1cm pieces

olive oil

1 teaspoon dried wild oregano

200g feta cheese, crumbled

1 small packet (about 30g) of fresh oregano, leaves roughly chopped

6 sheets of filo pastry

60g butter, melted

Maldon sea salt flakes and freshly ground black pepper

rocket salad, to serve

Preheat the oven to 220°C (200°C fan), Gas Mark 7. Line a large baking tray with baking paper.

Place the carrots on the lined tray. Drizzle with olive oil, season with salt and pepper and sprinkle over the dried oregano, then coat the carrot pieces evenly in the oil and seasonings. Spread out and roast for 30–35 minutes or until starting to brown and char around the edges. Remove from the oven and leave to cool.

Put the feta, fresh oregano, a generous amount of black pepper and the carrots into a large mixing bowl and mix together.

Line your large baking tray with fresh baking paper. Lay a filo sheet lengthways on a clean work surface or chopping board. Divide the carrot mixture into 6 equal portions. Form a portion into a long sausage shape near the bottom long edge of the filo, leaving a generous 2.5cm border clear at either end. Carefully, but very loosely, roll the pastry up to make a long cigar and seal the edge with melted butter. Coil the cigar into a snail shape without tightening the looseness of the pastry but squeezing and cupping it gently to keep it loose as you curve it round. Place on the lined tray and brush butter all over the exposed edges, trying to seal any broken bits using the butter and bits of pastry from the ends. Repeat with the remaining filo sheets and carrot mixture.

Bake for 22–25 minutes until nicely golden brown. Remove from the oven and serve with a rocket salad.

Serve with Tangy Pomegranate & Tomato Aubergines (see page 185).

Courgette, Lemon, Feta & Pine Nut Tart

This is one of those quick and easy recipes that can be thrown together in next to no time. No special skills or equipment are needed, just a little patience while the tart bakes and cools down enough for you to enjoy it. I love this kind of dish with a green leaf salad and a simple vinaigrette on the side, but you can also cut it into smaller portions and serve it as snacks or light bites with drinks, too.

SERVES 4

200g feta cheese, finely crumbled

250g ricotta cheese

1 teaspoon dried mint

1 teaspoon dried wild oregano

2 teaspoons lemon extract

finely grated zest of 1 unwaxed lemon

1 x 320g ready-rolled puff pastry sheet (about 350 x 230mm)

1 courgette, very thinly sliced

olive oil

handful of pine nuts

2 tablespoons clear honey

½ teaspoon pul biber chilli flakes (omit if you prefer)

Maldon sea salt flakes and freshly ground black pepper

Preheat the oven to 220°C (200°C fan), Gas Mark 7. Line a large baking tray with baking paper.

Put the feta, ricotta, dried herbs and lemon extract and zest into a mixing bowl with a good seasoning of salt and pepper and beat together until smooth.

Place the puff pastry sheet on the lined tray and score a 1cm-wide border around the edges, then spread the cheese mixture across the pastry up to the scored border.

Lay the courgette slices, slightly overlapping, on the cheese mixture, season well with salt and pepper and drizzle with olive oil. Scatter over the pine nuts and bake for 16–18 minutes until the pastry edges are nicely browned.

Remove from the oven and leave to cool slightly, then drizzle with the honey and sprinkle with the pul biber before serving.

Serve with Roasted Tomatoes with Labneh & Sumac Spice Oil (see page 177).

Curried Cheese & Potato Puffs

Bringing three of my favourite elements together – cheese, potatoes and pastry – seems a total no-brainer for a girl like me. But the really wonderful addition is the curry powder. It just works so well with the potato and cheese, and makes these little puffs absolutely irresistible – the ultimate snack.

MAKES 8

250g floury potatoes, peeled and
  halved if large
2 tablespoons medium curry powder
100g mature Cheddar cheese, grated
1 x 320g ready-rolled puff pastry sheet
  (about 350 x 230mm)

1 beaten egg or milk, for glazing
½ teaspoon nigella seeds
Maldon sea salt flakes and freshly
  ground black pepper
Sriracha or chilli sauce, to serve

Cook the potatoes in a saucepan of boiling water for 25–30 minutes or until cooked through. Drain and leave to cool completely.

Put the cooled potatoes into a mixing bowl, add the curry powder and a very generous amount of salt and pepper and mash into the potatoes, then mix in the cheese.

Divide the potato mixture into 8 portions and form each into a ball, then chill in the refrigerator for at least an hour.

Preheat the oven to 220°C (200°C fan), Gas Mark 7. Line a large baking tray with baking paper.

Cut the pastry sheet in half lengthways, then cut each half into 4 squares to make 8 in total. Place a ball of cheese and potato mixture on a pastry square, then work quickly to bring all 4 corners together in the centre, pinch the edges together and twist the tops to seal. Place on the lined tray. Repeat with the remaining cheese and potato mixture and pastry.

Brush all over with a little beaten egg or milk to glaze and sprinkle nigella seeds on top. Bake for 18 minutes until nicely browned, then serve with Sriracha or chilli sauce. These need no accompaniment.

Fatayer Puffs

When I want to feed people, I like to make a wide array of dishes including *fatayer*, but I don't always have time to make fresh pastry. So shop-bought pastry is the way forward and I rather like the lighter, flaky nature of puff pastry – the traditional *fatayer*, while perfectly delicious, has a chewier, somewhat weightier pastry dough. Now, I know the spice mix here looks excessive, but it is authentic, so do yourself a favour and double (or quadruple) the batch to save time when you next make these, because these little puffs are utterly delicious and you will definitely want to make them again.

MAKES 8

vegetable oil

250g minced lamb

1 heaped teaspoon garlic granules

¼ teaspoon paprika

¼ teaspoon ground cumin

¼ teaspoon ground coriander

¼ teaspoon ground cloves

¼ teaspoon ground cinnamon

⅛ teaspoon ground nutmeg

⅛ teaspoon cayenne pepper

½ small packet (about 15g) of flat leaf parsley, finely chopped

25g pine nuts

1 x 320g ready-rolled all-butter puff pastry sheet (about 350 x 230mm)

1 egg, beaten

Maldon sea salt flakes and freshly ground black pepper

Place a large frying pan over a high heat, add a little drizzle of vegetable oil followed by the minced lamb and immediately break it up as finely as possible to prevent it cooking in clumps. Continue cooking the mince, stirring as you go, until just cooked through but not browned. Add the garlic granules, all the spices and a generous amount of salt and pepper followed by the parsley and stir-fry for a further 5 minutes. Remove from the heat and leave to cool. Add the pine nuts and mix well.

Preheat the oven to 220°C (200°C fan), Gas Mark 7. Line a large baking tray with baking paper.

Cut the puff pastry sheet in half widthways, then cut each half into quarters to make 8 rectangles in total. Divide the lamb mixture into 8 equal portions. Form a portion into a mini sausage shape in the centre of a pastry rectangle, then pinch the pastry at either end and twist to seal and create mini boat shapes. Place on the lined tray. Repeat with the remaining lamb mixture and pastry rectangles. Brush the pastries with beaten egg to glaze and bake for 20–22 minutes, or until the pastry is golden brown. Remove from the oven and serve.

Serve with 'Hummus' Salad (see page 22).

Halloumi Airbags

Don't let the recipe title put you off because until you make them, you won't know what I mean. These lovely little halloumi and herb pastries inflate when you fry them, making them feather-light, crisp and delicious. They are best enjoyed freshly made, so fry them just before you intend to eat them.

MAKES 16

250g block of halloumi cheese,
    coarsely grated
1 small packet (about 30g) of flat leaf
    parsley, finely chopped
1 small packet (about 30g) of dill,
    finely chopped
2 teaspoons dried mint
vegetable oil, for frying
2 sheets of filo pastry (each about
    480 x 250mm)
1 egg, beaten
freshly ground black pepper

Put the halloumi, fresh herbs and dried mint into a mixing bowl with a generous amount of black pepper and mix together until well combined, then set aside.

Heat a large, deep frying pan over a medium-high heat, pour in about 2.5cm vegetable oil and bring to frying temperature (add a small piece of filo pastry: if it sizzles immediately, the oil is hot enough). Line a baking tray with a double layer of kitchen paper.

Cut each filo pastry sheet into 8 squares. Divide the halloumi mixture into 16 equal portions. Place a portion on a filo square, positioned diamond-wise, then brush 2 adjacent edges of the diamond with beaten egg, fold over the filling to form a triangle and press the edges together to seal. Repeat with the remaining halloumi mixture and filo squares. Pinch each airbag tightly around the edges.

Add the airbags to the hot oil and fry in batches for a minute on each side until they puff up and turn golden brown. Remove with a slotted spoon and transfer to the paper-lined plate to drain, then serve. These need no accompaniment.

Lamb & Coriander Dumplings

There isn't a single dumpling I couldn't love, whether fried, steamed or boiled, in sauce or soup – I adore them all. The filling I've created here is a punchy little number, but that is very much how I like it.

MAKES 18

vegetable oil, for frying

150g plain flour, plus extra for dusting

2–3 pinches of Maldon sea salt flakes, crumbled

125ml boiling water, or more if needed

1 tablespoon cumin seeds

½ teaspoon chilli flakes

250g minced lamb

½ small packet (about 15g) of fresh coriander, very finely chopped

1 tablespoon rice vinegar

2 garlic cloves, crushed

4 tablespoons cold water

Maldon sea salt flakes and freshly ground black pepper

Sriracha or light soy sauce, to serve

To make the dough, mix the flour and salt together in a mixing bowl, pour in the boiling water and mix with a fork until the mixture comes together into a dough, adding a little more boiling water if needed. Dust a work surface with a little extra flour and knead the dough for 2 minutes. Place back in the bowl, cover with clingfilm and leave to rest for 20 minutes.

Meanwhile, for the filling, heat a dry frying pan over a medium-high heat, add the cumin seeds and toast for 1–2 minutes until they release their aroma, shaking the pan intermittently to prevent them from burning. Remove from the heat and stir in the chilli flakes while still hot, then grind together using a pestle and mortar.

Put the remaining ingredients, except the vegetable oil, into a mixing bowl, add the ground cumin and chilli and season very well with salt and pepper. Then use your hands to work the ingredients together really well until you have an evenly combined smooth paste. Weigh the mixture and divide it into 18 equal portions.

Once the dough has rested, dust a tray with a little extra flour. Form the dough into one long sausage shape and divide into 18 balls. Roll out each ball into a circle about 8cm in diameter, place on the tray and cover with a clean damp tea towel until you need them.

To make the dumplings, place a portion of the lamb filling on a dough circle and fold one side of the dough over it to form a semicircle. Seal and crimp the edges by pressing with the tines of a fork. Stand them with the seam upright so they form a flat base. Repeat with the remaining dough circles and filling.

Heat a large frying pan over a medium-high heat, drizzle in some vegetable oil and fry half the dumplings for about 2–3 minutes until the bases start to turn golden. Pour in the cold water and shake the pan gently, place a lid on the pan and cook for 6–8 minutes until well browned and crispy on the base. Remove from the pan and repeat the process with the remaining dumplings. Serve with the dipping sauce of your choice.

Herb & Spice Feta,

These feta balls are simple enough to make, but I chose four different flavourings to give them a little extra dimension. Enjoy them in salads or even on their own with lovely warm pillowy bread that's good for mopping, or flatbreads or wraps. They also make a wonderful gift, so prepare a double batch if you think you can stand to part with a jar. Keep the feta submerged in oil in an unopened jar in the fridge for up to a week.

SERVES 2–4

200g block of feta cheese, cut into 12

1 teaspoon sumac

1½ teaspoons dried wild oregano

2 teaspoons pul biber chilli flakes

2 teaspoons nigella seeds

extra virgin olive oil

flatbread or wraps, to serve

Shape the feta pieces into balls using your hands, then roll three of the balls in one of the four spices until evenly coated all over. Repeat with the remaning balls and spices. Put them all on to a small serving plate, drizzle with extra virgin olive oil and serve with flatbread or wraps.

Alternatively, place the coated feta in a clean airtight jar, pour in enough of the oil to cover them and seal the lid tightly, then refrigerate until required.

Serve with Beetroot & Pomegranate Salad (see page 13) or My Platter of Dreams (see page 21).

Tamarind Chicken Wings

What can I say? I'm a sucker for chicken wings. I don't really know why wings do it for me like no other part of a chicken ever could, but the real bonus is that they are cheap and cheerful and – when cooked properly – can beat a fillet steak, in my humble opinion, any day. My favourite flavour profiles for wings are either spicy or sweet and sticky, though even better is the two aforementioned combined. Tamarind is one of those unapologetically sour ingredients from the East that is often misunderstood in the West, but balance out its sharpness with a little sweetness and it's wonderfully satisfying.

SERVES 4

1kg chicken wings

2 level tablespoons baking powder

Maldon sea salt flakes and freshly ground black pepper

2 spring onions, thinly sliced diagonally from root to tip, to garnish

For the sauce

3 tablespoons tamarind paste

2 tablespoons warm water

6 tablespoons clear honey

1 teaspoon pul biber chilli flakes, plus extra to garnish (optional)

Preheat the oven to 200°C (180°C fan), Gas Mark 6. Line your largest baking tray with baking paper.

Put the chicken wings into a mixing bowl, add the baking powder and a very generous amount of salt and pepper and massage really well into the wings as best you can. Spread the wings out on the lined tray and bake for 30 minutes, then increase the oven temperature to 270°C (250°C fan), Gas Mark 10 or your highest gas mark setting, and bake for a further 25 minutes until nicely browned and cooked through.

Meanwhile, place the sauce ingredients along with a gentle seasoning of salt in a small saucepan over a gentle heat and stir until evenly combined and gently bubbling. Remove from the heat and set aside.

Transfer the baked wings to a clean mixing bowl and pour over the sauce, ensuring you coat each wing. Serve garnished with the spring onions and a little extra pul biber if desired.

Serve with Spice-roasted Potatoes with Tomato, Pepper & Harissa Sauce (see page 166) or Nut Butter Noodles (see page 204).

Minced Lamb & Cheddar Tortillas

This is the kind of quick and easy food that everyone in my household loves. I've been blessed with stepkids who thankfully like spice, and these quesadilla-inspired filled tortillas are a big win for them and an even bigger relief for me. This recipe comes together quickly and can be eaten sliced for snacks, or with your favourite salads or veg to make a proper meal. Use any minced meat plus any cheese you like, but I do feel that the sharpness of a good mature Cheddar works really well with the spices here.

SERVES 2–4

vegetable oil

250g minced lamb

1 teaspoon garlic granules

1 teaspoon ground cumin

1 teaspoon paprika

2 tablespoons tomato purée

½ packet (about 15g) of flat leaf
   parsley, finely chopped

2 large tortilla wraps

100g mature Cheddar cheese, grated

Maldon sea salt flakes and freshly
   ground black pepper

For the harissa yogurt (optional)

150g Greek-style yogurt

1 tablespoon harissa

Place a frying pan over a high heat, add a little drizzle of vegetable oil followed by the minced lamb along with the garlic granules and all the spices and immediately break the mince up as finely as possible to prevent it cooking in clumps while you work in the flavourings. Add the tomato purée and a generous amount of salt and pepper and stir-fry for 5 minutes, then add the parsley and stir-fry for another couple of minutes until the mince is fully cooked. Set aside.

To make the harissa yogurt (if using), pour the yogurt into a small bowl and stir through the harissa just enough to create a marble effect. Set aside.

Heat a large frying pan over a medium heat, place a tortilla in the dry pan and scatter half the Cheddar on to the surface. Using a slotted spoon (to avoid any excess grease), add half the mince on to one half of the tortilla. Check that the underside of the tortilla is toasting nicely, and when ready, fold the half without the mince over the filling. Remove from the pan and repeat with the remaining ingredients. Cut the filled tortillas into portions and serve with the harissa yogurt if desired. These need no accompaniment.

Mushroom Cigar Börek

I do love the therapeutic element of making *sigara börek* – the gentle stuffing and rolling of them can be quite soothing, so long as you aren't in a hurry. While this filling is not a traditional one, mushrooms work well with spice and have their own distinctly earthy flavour, which is perfect as a meat alternative. I would usually brush my börek with beaten egg or butter for crunch, gloss and richness, but I wanted to keep this recipe friendly for people of every dietary description, so I used a little oil instead – it works just as well.

MAKES 16

500g chestnut mushrooms, halved
    and thinly sliced

olive oil

1 teaspoon garlic granules

2 teaspoons za'atar

1 teaspoon pul biber chilli flakes

4 sheets of filo pastry (each about
    480 x 250mm)

1 teaspoon nigella seeds

Maldon sea salt flakes and freshly
    ground black pepper

Heat a large frying pan over a medium-high heat, and once hot, add the mushrooms to the dry pan, allow them to release their liquid and then cook for 4–5 minutes until all the liquid has evaporated, stirring occasionally. Add a drizzle of olive oil followed by the garlic granules, spices and a good seasoning of salt and pepper and stir-fry for 3–4 minutes. Remove from the heat and leave to cool.

Preheat the oven to 220°C (200°C fan), Gas Mark 7. Line a large baking tray with baking paper.

Cut the filo pastry sheets in half widthways, then cut each in half to make 16 long strips in total. Divide the mushroom mixture into 16 equal portions. Pour 2–3 tablespoons olive oil into a little bowl and grab a pastry brush. Place a portion of the mushroom mixture near the bottom of a pastry strip, then fold the bottom edge up over the filling. Begin rolling up the pastry loosely. Once you have reached halfway, fold the sides of the pastry strip into the middle and continue rolling up. Seal the end of the pastry with a little oil and place the pastry cigar, seam-side down, on the lined baking tray. Repeat with the remaining mushroom mixture and filo strips.

Brush the pastry cigars all over with olive oil and scatter with the nigella seeds. Bake for 20–22 minutes, or until golden brown. Remove from the oven and leave to cool slightly before serving.

Serve with Mama Ghanoush (see page 158).

My Sweet, Salty & Sublime 'BHT

I never thought that combining two salty ingredients would work so well. Then I added juicy tomatoes and sweet harissa ketchup to bacon and halloumi, put it all in fresh pitta and it came together beautifully. No disrespect to the BLT, but the BHT is the kind of thing I could eat for breakfast, lunch and dinner – and it hits every spot it should.

SERVES 2

4 streaky bacon rashers

2 tomatoes, thin disc trimmed from the top and base of each, then cut into thick slices

1 teaspoon dried wild oregano

olive oil

250g block of halloumi cheese, cut into 6 slices

2 pitta breads

freshly ground black pepper

For the sauce

2 tablespoons tomato ketchup

1 tablespoon rose harissa

Line a plate with a double layer of kitchen paper. Heat a frying pan over a high heat and fry the bacon until crisp on both sides. Remove and transfer to the paper-lined plate to drain.

Wipe the pan clean and place over a medium-high heat. Season both sides of the tomato slices with the oregano and pepper, drizzle a little oil into the pan and fry for 1–2 minutes on each side until charred. Remove from the pan and set aside.

Drizzle a little more oil into the pan and fry the halloumi slices for a few minutes on both sides until deep golden brown.

Meanwhile, mix the sauce ingredients together in a small bowl.

Open up the pittas, divide the bacon, halloumi, tomatoes and then the sauce between them and serve. This needs no accompaniment.

Spicy Keema Rolls

The filling in these little rolls wouldn't be out of place in a samosa, and these are my way of satisfying any craving I might have for one. The recipe makes eight, but you could, of course, use a few more sheets of filo pastry and make them slightly smaller as part of a bigger feast. They also work really well with veggie mince, and if you prefer a vegan approach, you can ditch the egg in favour of water to bind the mixture and glaze them with oil instead. Serve with mango chutney or your favourite sweet dipping sauce.

MAKES 8

vegetable oil

1 large onion, finely chopped

1 teaspoon cumin seeds

500g minced beef

1 teaspoon ground turmeric

1 tablespoon pul biber chilli flakes

1 tablespoon garlic granules

generous handful of frozen peas

1 small packet (about 30g) of fresh coriander, finely chopped

4 sheets of filo pastry (each about 480 x 250mm)

1 egg, beaten

Maldon sea salt flakes and freshly ground black pepper

Preheat the oven to 220°C (200°C fan), Gas Mark 7. Line a large baking tray with baking paper.

Heat a large frying pan over a medium-high heat, drizzle in some vegetable oil and fry the onion until softened. Add the cumin seeds and continue frying until the onion is nicely browned.

Add the minced beef and break it up as finely as you can to prevent it cooking in clumps, folding it into the onion. Add the spices and garlic granules and a generous amount of salt and pepper and stir well. Continue cooking until the mince is just cooked through but not browned, stirring as you go, then stir in the peas and cook for a couple of minutes before adding the coriander and cooking for a couple more minutes. Remove from the heat and leave to cool.

Cut each filo pastry sheet in half widthways to make 8 squares in total. Divide the meat mixture into 8 equal portions. Place a portion near the bottom edge of a filo square, then fold in the sides and bottom edge up over the filling. Begin rolling up the pastry, tucking in the edges on each side as you go. Once you have reached halfway, brush the exposed pastry edge with beaten egg and finish rolling up, then seal the edge. Place, seam-side down, on the lined baking tray. Repeat with the rest of the meat mixture and filo squares. Brush with beaten egg to glaze and bake for 20–22 minutes, or until golden brown. Remove from the oven and serve.

Serve with Ras el Hanout & Sweet Potato with Tahini Yogurt & Herb Oil (see page 163) or Roasted Aubergines with Spicy Peanut Sauce (see page 173).

Sabich

I first heard of *sabich* (pronounced sab-eekh), an Iraqi–Jewish sandwich usually eaten for breakfast and now very popular in Israel, while filming a food show in Canada. This wonderful aubergine sandwich has all the makings of one of the greatest meatless sandwiches I have ever tasted. Traditionally, it is served with *amba* sauce, a sharp mango sauce that is hard to find, so I raided my store cupboard and dug out the mango chutney and added the sharp tang of lime juice, which did the job perfectly.

SERVES 4

3 aubergines, peeled and cut into
    1.5cm-thick slices

olive oil, for brushing

1 teaspoon ground cumin

1 teaspoon ground coriander

1 teaspoon garlic granules

½ cucumber, cut into 1cm cubes

2 tomatoes, diced

1 small red onion, halved and thinly
    sliced into half moons

½ packet (about 15g) of fresh
    coriander, roughly chopped

½ packet (about 15g) of mint,
    leaves roughly chopped

Maldon sea salt flakes and freshly
    ground black pepper

To serve

6 tablespoons mango chutney

juice of 1 lime

150g Greek-style yogurt

4 pitta breads

2 soft boiled eggs, halved

Preheat the oven to 200°C (180°C fan), Gas Mark 6. Line a large baking tray with baking paper.

Place the aubergine slices on the lined tray and brush both sides generously with olive oil. Mix the spices and garlic granules together, then sprinkle over both sides, season both sides with salt and pepper and pat the seasoning into the aubergine. Roast for 30 minutes without turning over.

Meanwhile, mix the cucumber, tomatoes, onion and herbs together with some salt and pepper in a bowl. Mix the mango chutney and lime juice together in a separate bowl.

To serve, season the yogurt with salt and pepper, then open up the pitta breads, spread with the yogurt and divide the roasted aubergines between each pitta, followed by the salad, mango sauce and half a soft boiled egg. Add a little extra yogurt to finish.

Serve with Beetroot & Pomegranate Salad (see page 13) or 'Hummus' Salad (see page 22).

Cod Flavour Bombs

These are exactly what they say they are . . . delightful little cod bites just bursting with flavour! I do love fish fritters, cakes, dumplings and the like, and I could eat a dozen of these in one sitting without any trouble. But to make more of a meal of them, pile them into hot dog buns or wraps with some salad and your favourite sauce for the ultimate satisfaction – try them with chilli sauce or mayo flavoured with harissa and lime.

SERVES 2–4

500g boneless, skinless cod loin (or other white fish), cut into about 2.5cm cubes

2 teaspoons ground coriander

2 teaspoons pul biber chilli flakes

2 teaspoons dried wild oregano

1 unwaxed lemon

vegetable oil, for frying

Maldon sea salt flakes and freshly ground black pepper

juice of ½ lemon (use the leftover lemon above)

For the batter

50g butter, melted and cooled

2 eggs

175g plain flour

1 teaspoon pul biber chilli flakes

1 teaspoon ground coriander

1 teaspoon dried wild oregano

225ml cold beer (or sparkling water)

To serve

lime wedges

your favourite sauce

Put the cod into a mixing bowl. Add the spices, oregano and a generous amount of salt and pepper. Finely grate over the zest of the lemon and add half the juice and mix well to coat the fish.

In another bowl, beat the melted butter and eggs together, then add the flour, spices, oregano and a generous amount of salt and pepper and pour over the beer (or sparkling water). Use a hand whisk to beat everything together gently until you have a smooth batter but without overbeating (otherwise the batter will be heavy).

Heat a deep frying pan over a medium-high heat, pour in about 2.5cm vegetable oil and bring to frying temperature (add a little bit of the batter: if it sizzles immediately, the oil is hot enough). Line a plate with a double layer of kitchen paper.

Dip each piece of cod in turn into the batter, then carefully lower into the hot oil and fry in batches for 2–3 minutes or until crispy and deep golden brown. Remove with a slotted spoon and transfer to the paper-lined plate to drain. Enjoy with a good squeeze of lime juice and your favourite sauce.

Serve with Curried Potato Salad (see page 38).

Spicy Prawn Fritters

I have always thought of prawns as a really useful and convenient ingredient to keep in the freezer – ready for making pastas, rice dishes, soups, dumplings and stir-fries. These prawn fritters are utterly delicious and ideal for snacking or served with drinks but also great as part of a bigger meal. They are really easy to make and don't take much effort or time to cook, which makes them the perfect go-to time and again when in a pinch. You can chop and change some of the ingredients to suit what you have at home because they are very versatile and work with a myriad of different spices and ingredients.

MAKES 18–20

240g fresh or frozen raw peeled prawns, defrosted if frozen and patted dry with kitchen paper

vegetable oil, for frying

1 small packet (about 30g) of fresh coriander, finely chopped

1 heaped teaspoon garlic granules

finely grated zest of 1 unwaxed lime, the zested lime cut into wedges to serve

1 heaped teaspoon pul biber chilli flakes

1 teaspoon cumin seeds

1 egg

2 tablespoons plain flour

1 teaspoon baking powder

5 spring onions, thinly sliced diagonally from root to tip

Maldon sea salt flakes and freshly ground black pepper

sweet chilli sauce, to serve

Put the prawns into a small food processor and briefly pulse until they are chopped but not minced to a paste. Transfer to a small mixing bowl.

Add all the remaining ingredients to the mixing bowl, season very generously with salt and pepper and mix together until you have an evenly combined paste.

Heat a deep frying pan over a medium-high heat, pour in about 2.5cm vegetable oil and bring to frying temperature (add a pinch of the mixture: if it sizzles immediately, the oil is hot enough). Line a plate with a double layer of kitchen paper.

Using 2 teaspoons, form the paste into little quenelles, carefully add to the hot oil and fry in batches for a minute or so on each side until golden brown. Remove with a slotted spoon and transfer to the paper-lined plate to drain. Enjoy with sweet chill sauce and the lime wedges for squeezing over.

Serve with Warm Harissa Broccoli & Black Rice Salad (see page 41).

Roasted Vegetable, Za'atar & Labneh Tartines

Good things can be born out of laziness and necessity. Not something Plato would say, but merely one of my own observations from many years spent in the kitchen creating meals that make me happy. This one-tray genius came to me while, you guessed it, recipe testing! I was after a quick lunch using leftover ingredients, and as I was time poor, having already spent a lot cooking, I threw them all on to the same baking tray and hoped for the best. And it worked! This is really very good, and because it's served with bread, it feels substantial and rewarding enough to make a proper meal.

MAKES 4

2 red onions, halved, then each half cut into 3 wedges

1 aubergine, peeled and cut into 4cm chunks

garlic oil

3 heaped tablespoons za'atar

150g baby plum tomatoes, halved

4 large slices of sourdough bread

300g labneh or thick Greek yogurt, strained

Maldon sea salt flakes and freshly ground black pepper

Preheat the oven to 220°C (200°C fan), Gas Mark 7. Line your largest baking tray with baking paper.

Place the onion wedges on one side of the lined tray and break them up a little, then add the aubergine chunks to other side. Drizzle both the onion and aubergine generously with garlic oil and sprinkle each with a heaped tablespoon of za'atar and a generous amount of black pepper, then use your hands to evenly coat them in the oil and seasonings.

Sit the tomatoes, cut-side up, on a different part of the tray, sprinkle with 1 heaped teaspoon of za'atar and season with pepper, but don't add any oil.

Roast for 30 minutes. Remove from the oven, season with salt and set aside.

Toast the sourdough bread in a toaster, then divide the labneh or yogurt between each slice and top with a portion of the roasted vegetables, plus an extra seasoning using the remaining za'atar if desired. This needs no accompaniment.

Bean & Feta Patties

These lovely little patties are quick and easy to make, and you can serve them in a multitude of ways. I wholeheartedly recommend following the serving suggestion below, but – to give you another simple option – I love serving them as sliders, with mini burger buns, lettuce and tomato slices on the side. They are also excellent tucked into wraps.

MAKES 12

400g can cannellini beans, drained and rinsed

1 teaspoon ground turmeric

1 teaspoon pul biber chilli flakes

1 teaspoon cumin seeds

4 spring onions, thinly sliced from root to tip, 1 reserved for garnish

handful of chopped flat leaf parsley

100g feta cheese, crumbled

vegetable oil, for frying

Maldon sea salt flakes and freshly ground black pepper

To serve

3–4 tablespoons Greek-style yogurt

3–4 tablespoons pomegranate molasses or sweet tamarind sauce

50g pomegranate seeds

Put the beans into a mixing bowl and mash them to a smooth paste. Add the spices, 3 of the spring onions and the parsley and mix together well. Add a very generous seasoning of salt and pepper followed by the feta and gently combine without mashing the feta.

Place a large frying pan over a medium-high heat and drizzle in enough oil to coat the base of the pan. Divide the mixture into 12 equal balls (to be as precise as possible, you can weigh the mixture and divide it) and then gently flatten the balls into patties. Once the oil is hot, fry the patties, in batches if necessary, for a couple of minutes on each side until deeply golden brown. Beware that the patties are soft and may break if not handled carefully, so use a spatula to carefully flip them over and then remove them from the pan.

Serve on a platter drizzled with the yogurt and pomegranate molasses or sweet tamarind sauce, and scattered with the reserved spring onion and pomegranate seeds.

Serve with Pan-fried Salmon with Barberry Butter (see page 133).

Halloumi & Avocado Wraps with Harissa Ketchup

I always have halloumi in my refrigerator and I have tried many versions of halloumi sandwiches, from pittas and toasties to baps and burgers, but this wrap is one of my favourites. The harissa ketchup really makes this wrap so flavoursome and it is such a quick and comforting lunch or dinner.

MAKES 2

olive oil

250g block of halloumi cheese, cut into 8 slices

1 tablespoon dried wild oregano

2 large tortilla wraps

1 large tomato, cut in half, then cut into half moons

½ small red onion, cut in half, then thinly sliced into half moons

4 Baby Gem lettuce leaves

1 avocado, halved, stone removed and cut into slices

3–4 tablespoons Greek-style yogurt

For the harissa ketchup

1 heaped tablespoon harissa

3 tablespoons tomato ketchup

Heat a dry frying pan over a medium-high heat (medium heat if using a gas hob).

Drizzle a little olive oil on both sides of the halloumi slices. Once the pan is hot, fry the halloumi for 3 minutes or so on each side until nicely browned and somewhat soft.

Sprinkle a quarter of the oregano on each wrap, then add 4 slices of cooked halloumi to each wrap. Layer the tomato, onion, lettuce and avocado on top of the halloumi.

Add dollops of yogurt over the salad. Mix the harissa with the ketchup until evenly combined and drizzle over, then sprinkle the remaining oregano on top. Fold up the wraps and serve. This needs no accompaniment.

Sweet Potato & Chickpea Balls

Inspired by my love for falafels, these are quite different and much lighter than the source of their inspiration. Serving them with salad on the side is wonderful, but I also like piling them into wraps with harissa yogurt or into white rolls with some yogurt, mango chutney and a squeeze of lime juice.

MAKES 18–20

500g sweet potatoes, unpeeled

400g can chickpeas, well drained and patted dry

1 small onion, very finely chopped

1 teaspoon ground cumin

1 teaspoon pul biber chilli flakes

1 teaspoon ground coriander

½ teaspoon ground cinnamon

2 garlic cloves, minced

3 tablespoons plain flour

1 teaspoon baking powder

½ small packet (about 15g) of fresh coriander, very finely chopped

1 tablespoon black and white sesame seeds

1 teaspoon nigella seeds

Maldon sea salt flakes and freshly ground black pepper

pitta breads, to serve

For the harissa yogurt (optional)

150g Greek-style or plant-based yogurt

1 tablespoon harissa

Preheat the oven to 200°C (180°C fan), Gas Mark 6. Line a baking tray with baking paper. Place the sweet potatoes on the lined tray and roast for an hour. Remove from the oven and leave to cool, then peel away the skins.

Tip the well-drained chickpeas into a large mixing bowl. Using a masher, meat hammer or the end of a rolling pin, mash as finely as possible. Add the cooked sweet potato flesh, onion, spices, garlic, flour, baking powder, a generous amount of salt and pepper and lastly the fresh coriander, and mix together well.

Line your baking tray with fresh baking paper. Roll the mixture into 18–20 balls and place on the lined tray. Mix the sesame seeds with the nigella seeds and scatter over each ball. Chill in the refrigerator for an hour.

Meanwhile, pour the yogurt into a small bowl (if using) and stir through the harissa just enough to create a marble effect.

When ready to bake, preheat the oven to 220°C (200°C fan), Gas Mark 7. Bake the balls for 12–14 minutes until nicely browned. Remove from the oven and leave to cool for a few minutes so that they firm up slightly, then serve with pitta breads and the harissa yogurt if desired.

Serve with Roasted Aubergines with Spicy Peanut Sauce (see page 173).

Meat, Poultry, Fish & Seafood,

Chicken, Apricot, Orange & Almond Tagine

Tagines are that wonderful marriage of meat or vegetables with sweet and spiced flavour pairings. What you put into yours is entirely up to you and may be dependent on traditions, local and seasonal availability, and personal preference, of course. I like my tagines to have lots of texture and layers of deep flavour not just from meat but also from dried fruits, nuts and fresh herbs. This particular combination can perhaps be called the sweeter cousin of the classic chicken, olive and preserved lemon, turning away from the wonderfully sour character of the lemon to the more gently acidic profile of orange and that irresistible, almost syrupy, sweet chewiness of dried apricots, plumped from absorbing the broth of the tagine.

SERVES 6–8

vegetable oil

2 large onions, roughly chopped

1kg bone-in, skinless chicken thighs

6 fat garlic cloves, thinly sliced

1 heaped teaspoon cumin seeds

1 teaspoon ground cinnamon

1 teaspoon paprika

1 teaspoon ground ginger

½ teaspoon cayenne pepper

finely grated zest and juice of
   1 unwaxed orange

1 tablespoon clear honey

150g dried apricots

50g whole blanched almonds

Maldon sea salt flakes and freshly
   ground black pepper

½ small packet (about 15g) of flat leaf
   parsley, leaves roughly chopped,
   to garnish

Place a large saucepan over a medium-high heat, add a drizzle of vegetable oil and fry the onions until softened and translucent. Add the chicken thighs and garlic and stir well. Mix in the spices, stir and cook for a few minutes before adding the orange zest and juice, honey and a generous amount of salt and pepper, then cook for a further 5 minutes, stirring occasionally.

Pour over enough boiling water to just about cover the ingredients, reduce to a gentle medium heat and cook, uncovered, for 1½ hours, stirring occasionally. Stir in the dried apricots and cook for a further 30 minutes.

Meanwhile, preheat the oven to 220°C (200°C fan), Gas Mark 7. Spread the almonds out on a baking tray and toast for 8 minutes. Remove from the oven and leave to cool.

When the tagine is ready, serve scattered with the toasted almonds and parsley.

Serve with Cheat's Zereshk Polow (see page 195).

Herb Koftas with Warm Yogurt Sauce & Spiced Mint Butter

While this isn't a Turkish recipe, a lot of what I create is inspired by flavours and techniques used in Turkish, Persian and Middle Eastern cuisines. I prefer to make smallish meatballs for this recipe, but you can make them bigger if you like. These are lovely served with small pasta shapes, such as orzo, or rice or pillowy bread.

MAKES 35–40
MEATBALLS/
SERVES 4–6

500g minced lamb

6 spring onions, thinly sliced from root to tip, 2 reserved for garnish

2 fat garlic cloves, minced

1 heaped teaspoon pul biber chilli flakes

1 heaped teaspoon paprika

1 heaped teaspoon dried mint

1 small packet (about 30g) of flat leaf parsley, finely chopped, some reserved for garnish

1 small packet (about 30g) of dill, finely chopped, some reserved for garnish

½ teaspoon bicarbonate of soda

vegetable oil, for frying

250g Greek yogurt

Maldon sea salt flakes and freshly ground black pepper

For the butter

50g butter

1 teaspoon dried mint

1 teaspoon pul biber chilli flakes

Put the minced lamb, spring onions, garlic, spices, dried mint, fresh herbs and bicarbonate of soda into a mixing bowl and season very generously with salt and pepper. Use your hands to work the ingredients together really well until you have an evenly combined smooth paste, then roll the mixture into 35–40 balls.

Heat a drizzle of oil in a large frying pan over a medium-high heat. Line a plate with a double layer of kitchen paper. Once the pan is hot, add the meatballs and fry on one side for 3–4 minutes, then turn and fry on the other side for 3–4 minutes before shaking the pan to finish frying the other sides.

Meanwhile, put the yogurt into a saucepan, season with salt and pepper and heat gently (to avoid curdling) until hot, then remove from the heat.

Melt the butter with the dried mint and pul biber in a small saucepan.

Once the meatballs are cooked, transfer to the paper-lined plate to drain, then place them on a platter, pour over the yogurt and drizzle with the butter. Scatter with the reserved spring onions and chopped herbs to serve.

Serve with Tomato & Feta Fritters (see page 181).

Dried Lime & Spice Marinated Lamb Chops

It seems few cultures embrace sour flavourings quite the way we Persians and some Arabs do. Dried white limes are funny little things. To the untrained eye, these wrinkled, ugly little dried-up limes look like they need throwing away, but as you'll discover, they possess a wealth of flavour and a marvellous acidity that can be used in many dishes in different ways. I must admit that I was an adult before I first saw dried black limes – and I was shocked! We Persians don't tend to use them, but now I buy them when I can to either prick and add to stews whole or – better still – crush and grind to make a spectacular souring agent that can be added to everything from soups and stews to marinades and cocktails. Here they bring a citrus kick that's absolutely wonderful with lamb.

SERVES 2

3 dried limes (white or black)

1 teaspoon cumin seeds, toasted in a dry pan for 1–2 minutes

2 teaspoons garlic granules

1 teaspoon paprika

3 tablespoons olive oil

juice of ½ lime

4 lamb chops

Maldon sea salt flakes and freshly ground black pepper

To serve

steamed white rice

chopped tomatoes

finely sliced red onion

chopped parsley leaves

Preheat your oven to its highest setting. Line a baking tray with baking paper.

Put the dried limes and toasted cumin seeds into a spice grinder or bullet blender and blitz together until finely ground to a powder, or use a pestle and mortar. Transfer to a mixing bowl, add all the remaining ingredients, except the lamb, and season well with salt and pepper. Mix into a paste, then rub all over both sides of the lamb chops.

Place the lamb chops on the lined tray and roast for 14–16 minutes, depending how hot your oven goes and the thickness of the lamb, until cooked through to your liking. Remove from the oven and serve immediately with plain white rice and a tomato, onion and parsley salad.

Serve with Traybaked Spicy Chickpeas & Aubergines with Yogurt & Herbs (see page 174) or Dampokhtak (see page 196).

Lamb, Dried Fig & Preserved Lemon Tagine

Box-ticking all the crucial elements I love in a good tagine, this flavoursome combination, though not authentic, marries together sweet, sour, spicy and crunchy components. I like to use lamb neck fillets, but boneless lamb shoulder is another option if you prefer. The warm spices in tagines are a flavour explosion, and while often sweet, there is always a contrasting sharp element that creates perfect balance. Here, preserved lemons come into play and, for a fruitier burst of sharpness, I've added barberries. Hazelnuts provide the crunch.

SERVES 6–8

olive oil

2 large onions, roughly chopped

800g lamb neck fillets, cut into 2.5cm chunks

1 head of garlic, cloves separated, peeled and kept whole

1 heaped teaspoon ground cumin

1 teaspoon ground cinnamon

1 teaspoon ground turmeric

2 tablespoons clear honey

300g dried figs, some whole, some halved

2 tablespoons dried barberries

4 preserved lemons, deseeded and each cut into 3–4 thick slices

50g blanched hazelnuts, chopped

Maldon sea salt flakes and freshly ground black pepper

½ small packet (about 15g) of flat leaf parsley, roughly chopped, to garnish

Place a large saucepan over a medium-high heat, add a drizzle of olive oil and fry the onions until softened and translucent. Add the lamb and garlic cloves and stir well. Mix in the spices, stir and cook for a few minutes before adding the honey and a generous amount of salt and pepper, mix well, then cook for a further 10–15 minutes, stirring occasionally.

Pour over enough boiling water to just about cover the ingredients, reduce to a gentle medium heat and cook, uncovered, for 1½ hours, stirring occasionally.

Stir in the figs, barberries and preserved lemons and cook for a further 30 minutes.

Meanwhile, preheat the oven to 220°C (200°C), Gas Mark 7. Spread the hazelnuts out on a baking tray and toast for 8 minutes – check after 6 minutes to ensure they do not burn. Remove from the oven, leave to cool, then roughly chop.

Taste and adjust the seasoning of the tagine if desired, then sprinkle with the parsley and hazelnuts and serve.

Serve with Cheat's Zereshk Polow (see page 195).

My Tender TFC

The turmeric spice here reminds me of the famous yellow-tinged fried chicken of Malaysia, but the buttermilk has been borrowed from the Americans as a tenderizer. Buttered corn on the cob makes a perfect accompaniment.

SERVES 4–6

1kg bone-in, skin-on chicken thighs
    and drumsticks
vegetable oil, for deep-frying
Maldon sea salt flakes and freshly
    ground black pepper
4–6 sweetcorn cobs, cooked, to serve
    (optional)

For the coating
200g plain flour
3 tablespoons ground turmeric
1 tablespoon garlic granules
½ teaspoon cayenne pepper

For the marinade
300ml buttermilk
1 tablespoon ground turmeric
1 tablespoon garlic granules
1 teaspoon paprika
1 teaspoon coriander
½ teaspoon cayenne pepper

Mix the marinade ingredients together in a large mixing bowl. Add the chicken and a generous amount of salt and pepper, then use your hands to mix everything together well and ensure all the chicken is evenly coated all over. Cover the bowl with clingfilm and leave to marinate in the refrigerator for at least 4 hours or overnight.

When you are ready to fry, mix the coating ingredients and a generous amount of salt and pepper together in another bowl.

Heat a large, deep saucepan over a medium-high heat, pour in about 7.5cm vegetable oil and bring to frying temperature (add a breadcrumb: if it sizzles immediately, the oil is hot enough). Put a double layer of kitchen paper on a large plate and set aside.

Using tongs, take a piece of chicken out of the marinade, roll in the coating mixture until well coated and carefully lower into the hot oil. Fry the chicken in batches for 15–20 minutes, or until the chicken is crisp and nicely golden brown and cooked through. Remove from the pan and leave to drain on the kitchen paper while you cook the second batch. Leave for a minute or two before serving with corn on the cob if desired.

Serve with Curried Potato Salad (see page 38) or Warm Orzo, Black-eyed Bean & Herb Salad (see page 42).

My Ultimate Mince & Aubergines

The combination of minced meat and aubergines is popular in so many cuisines in the East and for good reason – it's an absolute winner! This is the perfect dish to serve with just some flatbread on the side, as it has everything you could possibly want already. While you could bake the aubergines if you prefer – after brushing with the spiced oil, bake on a baking paper-lined baking tray for 25–30 minutes in the oven preheated to 200°C (180°C fan), Gas Mark 6 – frying does make them more supple and delicious. Your call! I am all for making my recipes fit in with your preferences . . . just be sure to try this one because it is the perfect dish.

SERVES 2–4

1 teaspoon paprika

1 teaspoon ground cumin

4 tablespoons garlic oil

1 large aubergine, cut into 1cm-thick slices (about 8–9)

For the topping

250g minced beef

1 heaped tablespoon rose harissa

1 teaspoon garlic granules

150g Greek yogurt

handful of chopped flat leaf parsley

pomegranate molasses, for drizzling

Maldon sea salt flakes

Heat a large frying pan over a medium heat. Mix the spices with the garlic oil, then brush both sides of the aubergine slices with the spiced oil. Once the pan is hot, add the aubergine slices and cook for 8 minutes or so on each side until soft and deeply browned. Remove from the pan and set aside covered loosely with foil to keep warm.

Increase the heat under the frying pan to high, add the minced beef along with the harissa, garlic granules and a good seasoning of salt and immediately break it up as finely as you can to prevent it cooking in clumps. Continue cooking the mince, stirring as you go, until brown and fully cooked.

Arrange the aubergine slices on a serving platter and top and surround with the mince, then dollop with the yogurt, sprinkle with the parsley and drizzle with pomegranate molasses. Serve immediately.

Serve with Beetroot & Pomegranate Salad (see page 13) or Spice-roasted Potatoes with Tomato, Pepper & Harissa Sauce (see page 166).

Minced Lamb Börek

My first trip to Turkey was over 20 years ago, visiting my best friend Aysegul and her family in Istanbul. I remember 12 Turkish women in the family gathered to show me different recipes, beginning with choosing the right meat at the butchers and how to cut and grind it, to the techniques for rolling stuffed leaves and layering börek – it was an experience I will cherish. This recipe is based on the traditional Turkish *kıymalı börek*. I've using filo instead of the traditional (often homemade) *yufka* pastry and a little sprinkle of nigella seeds. I always say go-big-or-go-home, so this recipe also provides a more generous filling.

SERVES 7–9

500g minced lamb (20% fat)

vegetable oil

1 large onion, very finely chopped

50g butter, melted

8 sheets of filo pastry

50ml milk

pinch of nigella seeds

Maldon sea salt flakes and
   freshly ground black pepper

Remove the minced lamb from the refrigerator 30 minutes before cooking to come up to room temperature.

Preheat the oven to 220°C (200°C fan), Gas Mark 7. Select a 26cm round ovenproof dish (or anything of similar volume, whether square or rectangular).

Place a frying pan over a medium heat, drizzle in some vegetable oil and fry the onion until soft and translucent but without colouring. Add the minced lamb and immediately break it up as finely as possible to prevent it cooking in clumps and ensure it spreads evenly in the börek. Don't brown the meat or cook it over a high heat because you want it to remain soft and tender in every bite. Continue cooking the mince, stirring as you go, until fully cooked, then season generously with salt and pepper, stir well and set aside.

Brush the bottom of your ovenproof dish with melted butter. Arrange 2 filo pastry sheets in the dish overlapping if necessary so they completely cover the base and sides, then brush with melted butter. Divide the mince into 3 equal portions and spread one portion evenly on top of the filo base. Cover with another 2 filo pastry sheets and generously brush them with milk so they are visibly wet. Repeat the layering of mince and filo pastry sheets brushed with milk until you reach the final layer of mince. Fold the loose edges of filo over the mince, then lay the final 2 filo pastry sheets on top, overlapping if necessary so they cover the mince, and brush the remaining butter over all the pastry and sides, then tuck the edges down inside the dish.

Sprinkle over the nigella seeds and bake for 25 minutes or until nicely golden on top, then serve.

Serve with Burnt Courgettes with Lemon & Feta Yogurt (see page 145) or Mama Ghanoush (see page 158).

Crispy Sticky Harissa Lamb

Cantonese crispy shredded chilli beef is one of my all-time favourite dishes and this is very much my own creation and my nod to that wonderful combination of sweet and sticky, crispy and chewy bites of meat but using lamb and adding peppers to the mix instead of carrots. It's an explosion of flavour that ticks every box.

SERVES 3–4

6 tablespoons cornflour

350g lamb leg steaks, cut into
    1cm-wide strips

vegetable oil, for frying

1 large onion, halved and thinly sliced
    into half moons

1 red pepper, cored, deseeded and cut
    into very thin strips

5 spring onions, thinly sliced from
    root to tip, reserve some for garnish

Maldon sea salt flakes and freshly
    ground black pepper

steamed white rice, to serve

For the sauce

5 tablespoons clear honey

4 tablespoons rose harissa

3 tablespoons rice vinegar

2 tablespoons light soy sauce

2 tablespoons cornflour

Mix the cornflour with a very generous amount of salt and pepper in a mixing bowl, add the strips of lamb and really work the cornflour into the lamb for a minute or so. Set aside.

Heat a large frying pan over a medium-high heat, pour in about 2.5cm vegetable oil and bring to frying temperature (add a little bit of a lamb strip: if it sizzles immediately, the oil is hot enough). Line a plate with a double layer of kitchen paper.

While the oil is heating up, place a small saucepan over a medium heat, add all the sauce ingredients and whisk together until no lumps of cornflour remain and the mixture is smooth. Heat the sauce through but do not let it bubble or burn, then remove from the heat.

Fry the lamb strips in batches in the hot oil for about 2–3 minutes, or until very crisp on the outside. Remove with a slotted spoon and transfer to the paper-lined plate to drain.

Heat another large frying pan over a high heat, add a drizzle of vegetable oil and stir-fry the onion and red pepper until browned a little. Add the lamb strips followed by the sauce and toss together until evenly coated with the sauce, then add the spring onions and combine well. Serve immediately scattered with the reserved spring onions and alongside steamed white rice. This needs no accompaniment.

Nargessi Kofta Loaf

Nargessi kofta is the recipe from which the British Scotch egg may well have derived. Fortnum & Mason department store in London claims to have created the Scotch egg in 1738 as a picnic food, but its origins are likely to have been in dishes experienced by the British during their time in India. Even further back than this, the recipe is thought to have been brought to India by Persian cooks who came to the Mughal courts. Essentially, it's a kofta. This is my version, inspired by the flavours of Persia, containing whole boiled eggs. Simply put, this is a wonderfully juicy meatloaf recipe unlike any other.

SERVES 4–6

4 eggs

500g minced lamb

1 large onion, very finely chopped

75g dried apricots, each cut into 4 or 5 strips

50g pistachio nuts, roughly chopped

2 tablespoons dried barberries

2 tablespoons tomato purée

1 teaspoon bicarbonate of soda

1 teaspoon ground turmeric

2 teaspoons garlic granules

½ small packet (about 15g) of flat leaf parsley, finely chopped

½ small packet (about 15g) of fresh coriander, finely chopped

Maldon sea salt flakes and freshly ground black pepper

Preheat the oven to 180°C (160°C fan), Gas Mark 4. Line the base of a 900g/2lb loaf tin with baking paper.

Cook 3 of the eggs in a small saucepan of boiling water for 6 minutes, then drain, cool under cold running water, shell and set aside.

Put all the remaining ingredients, including the other egg (to bind) and a generous amount of salt and pepper, into a mixing bowl and use your hands to work the ingredients together really well for a couple of minutes until you have an evenly combined paste.

Divide the mixture in half and place the first half in the tin. Arrange the boiled eggs lengthways down the centre and then lay the rest of the mixture on top, being extra gentle so that you don't burst the eggs. Smooth the surface and make sure it is completely sealed. Bake for 40 minutes.

Remove the loaf from the oven and leave to sit for 5 minutes. Then using a non-metal utensil such as a spatula to ensure the edges come out cleanly, flip the loaf on to a large plate, cut into slices and serve.

Serve with Roasted Vegetable & Mixed Bean Salad with Herb Dressing (see page 33) or Warm Orzo, Black-eyed Bean & Herb Salad (see page 42).

Ras el Hanout & Orange Lamb Cutlet Platter

Cutlets would be the cut of lamb (my favourite meat) that I would go for if I had to choose just one. They have the perfect amount of fat and bone and a wonderful eye of meat, which makes their proportions ideal for marinating, grilling, barbecuing and roasting. This is very much a complete meal of a recipe that needs little else. It feels almost celebratory, but don't let that stop you from enjoying it whenever you like. The spiced components when brought together create a real explosion of flavour, one you'll want to experience again and again.

SERVES 3–4

8–10 well-trimmed lamb cutlets

3–4 tablespoons garlic oil

2 tablespoons ras el hanout

finely grated zest of 1 unwaxed orange and juice of ½

Maldon sea salt flakes and freshly ground black pepper

For the potatoes

1.5kg potatoes, peeled and cut into about 4cm chunks

3 tablespoons ghee (or vegetable oil if you prefer)

8 fat garlic cloves, thinly sliced

2 tablespoons dried fenugreek leaves

2 teaspoons cumin seeds

2 teaspoons ground turmeric

1 teaspoon chilli flakes (omit if you prefer)

100ml cold water

1 small packet (about 30g) of flat leaf parsley, leaves roughly chopped

For the aubergines

3 small or 2 large aubergines, peeled, halved lengthways and cut roughly into 3cm chunks

about 5–6 tablespoons garlic oil

2 teaspoons paprika

To serve

200g Greek yogurt

sweet tamarind sauce, for drizzling

75g pistachio slivers (or very roughly chopped whole nuts)

75g pomegranate seeds

continued overleaf

Put the lamb cutlets into a shallow bowl or dish, add the garlic oil, ras el hanout, orange zest and juice and a generous amount of salt, then rub evenly all over them. Cover the bowl or dish with clingfilm and leave to marinate at room temperature while you cook the aubergines and potatoes.

Preheat the oven to 220°C (200°C fan), Gas Mark 7. Line your largest baking tray with baking paper.

Place the aubergine chunks on the lined tray and drizzle over the garlic oil. Sprinkle with the paprika and a good amount of salt, then use your hands to evenly coat the chunks in the oil and spice. Spread out in a single layer and roast for about 25 minutes until nicely browned and starting to char around the edges. Remove from the oven and set aside.

Meanwhile, parboil the potatoes in a saucepan of boiling water for 10 minutes, then tip into a colander to drain. Return the pan to a low-medium heat, add the ghee (or vegetable oil), garlic slices, fenugreek leaves and spices and fry for a few minutes, ensuring they don't burn. Pour in the water and stir, then add the parboiled potatoes with a generous amount of salt and pepper and mix until evenly coated in the spices and garlic. Cover the pan with a lid and cook gently for about 20 minutes, stirring occasionally to prevent sticking.

Pop the aubergines back in the oven to reheat gently. Then check the potatoes, which should be a little browned when done and cooked through. Stir through the chopped parsley, reserving a little for a garnish.

Heat a frying pan over a medium-high heat and cook the marinated lamb chops for 2–3 minutes on each side. Remove from the pan and leave to rest while you get ready to serve.

Transfer the potatoes to a very large serving platter, then add the aubergines and sprinkle over the remaining parsley. Arrange the lamb cutlets on top. Lastly, dollop with the yogurt, drizzle with sweet tamarind sauce and finish with the pistachios and pomegranate seeds. This needs no accompaniment.

Persian Dolmeh-e barg

This recipe from my childhood is very dear to my heart, but not having the original recipe, I taught myself and experimented for many years to get it right so that the flavours matched my memories. *Dolmeh* is the Persian word for dolma, and we Persians eat the same filling in both stuffed vine leaves (*barg e moo*) as well as in onions, tomatoes, peppers and cabbage leaves. Rather than cigar shapes, our *dolmeh* are fashioned to look almost like plump teabags, which I think makes them infinitely less fiddly and a lot more substantial and satisfying. They are traditionally cooked on a stove, but I have found that baking ensures they cook through evenly. If you can, make them the day before eating, as they really do benefit from overnight resting and refrigeration, and a gentle reheating the next day.

MAKES 25–30

vegetable oil

1 large onion, finely chopped

250g minced lamb

1 small packet (about 30g) of fresh
   coriander, finely chopped

1 small packet (about 30g) of flat leaf
   parsley, finely chopped

1 small packet (about 30g) of chives,
   thinly sliced

3 tablespoons dried dill

1 teaspoon ground turmeric

50g uncooked yellow split peas

200g basmati rice

1 bunch of spring onions, thinly
   sliced from root to tip

1 packet or jar of vine leaves packed in
   brine, drained

Maldon sea salt flakes and freshly
   ground black pepper

For the tomato liquid

500ml boiling water

100g caster sugar

2 heaped tablespoons tomato purée

juice of 1 lemon

1 tablespoon olive oil

continued overleaf

Pour all the ingredients for the tomato liquid into a jug, stir together until the sugar has dissolved, then set aside.

Place a large frying pan over a medium-high heat, drizzle in some vegetable oil and fry the onion until soft and translucent. Add the minced lamb along with all the herbs, turmeric and a generous amount of salt and pepper and immediately break it up as finely as you can to prevent it cooking in clumps. Then add the split peas, rice and spring onions and cook gently for 10–15 minutes, stirring gently so as not to break the rice grains. Remove from the heat and leave to cool completely.

Preheat the oven to 180°C (160°C fan), Gas Mark 4.

Place a dessertspoonful of the meat filling on a vine leaf and roll up into a little fat parcel shape (think teabag size) – how you roll or seal the parcels really doesn't matter, and broken leaves can be overlaid with another leaf. Repeat until all the meat filling is used up.

Take a large ovenproof dish and line the base with vine leaves (if you don't have enough, use a double layer of foil or baking paper). Arrange the dolmeh, seam-side down and tightly packed, in the lined dish, then pour over the tomato liquid and cover with a double layer of foil. Bake for 2 hours, then remove the foil and bake for a further 30 minutes. Remove from the oven and leave to cool. These are best made the day before eating to allow the flavours to intensify, so refrigerate them until you are ready to serve the next day.

To reheat, preheat the oven to 180°C (160°C fan) Gas Mark 4. Place the dolmeh in an ovenproof dish, add a splash of water, then cover with foil. Reheat for 20–25 minutes, or until warmed through. These are best eaten warm rather than piping hot.

Serve with Burnt Courgettes with Lemon & Feta Yogurt (see page 145) or Roasted Tomatoes with Labneh & Sumac Spice Oil (see page 177).

Spiced Lamb & Potato Stew

I absolutely love Massamun (meaning 'Muslim') curry – a recipe thought to have Persian roots, thanks to Persian traders bringing influences and ingredients of their own on their travels to South East Asia. While this recipe is not remotely like a Massamun curry, it does include many of the same comforting notes and flavours, and can easily be recreated at home and all in one pot. For me, the combination of sweet and spice works so well in curries and stews that I find it incredibly hard to resist. You can also substitute beef shin for the lamb if you like. I like to serve this with plain boiled rice or bread.

SERVES 6

3 tablespoons vegetable oil

2 onions, halved and thinly sliced into
   half moons

1 tablespoon cumin seeds

1 tablespoon ground cumin

2 black cardamom pods

1 tablespoon ground cinnamon

1 teaspoon ground turmeric

½ teaspoon chilli flakes

2 star anise

2 tablespoons caster sugar

2 tablespoons rose harissa

800g boneless lamb shoulder, cut into
   2.5cm cubes

6 fat garlic cloves, peeled and kept
   whole

500g baby new potatoes

400ml can coconut milk

2 handfuls of salted peanuts

Maldon sea salt flakes and freshly
   ground black pepper

plain boiled rice or bread to serve

Place a large saucepan over a medium-high heat, add the vegetable oil and fry the onions until soft and beginning to brown. Add all the spices, sugar and rose harissa and mix really well until evenly combined. Cook for a few minutes, stirring regularly to prevent burning.

Add the lamb and garlic cloves along with a generous amount of salt and pepper and turn to coat the meat in the onion and spice mixture, then cook for a few minutes. Pour over enough boiling water to almost cover the ingredients, stir the contents of the pan again and reduce to a medium heat. Cover the pan with a lid and cook for 2 hours, stirring occasionally to prevent sticking.

Remove the lid, stir again and mix in the potatoes and coconut milk, then cook, uncovered, for a further hour. Check the amount of liquid and add a little more water if needed (it should be a rich sauce, but not watery), taste and adjust the seasoning if desired, then serve with the peanuts scattered on top. Serve with rice or bread. This needs no accompaniment.

Torsh̦e Shami

These little *shamis* came into my life when I was kid – I remember tasting them thinking they were the usual Persian *shamis* (a simple unspiced patty of mashed chickpeas and lamb with a hole poked through the centre), and at first bite I had the shock of my life! They were spicy and salty, then this insane burst of sour hit and, well, I was completely hooked. The word *torsh* means 'sour' in Persian. They are unlike anything I've ever tasted, and to this day they hold a special place in my heart. This recipe is more Iraqi than Persian, as my grandmother's sister was married to an Iraqi and I grew up eating food from both cuisines. These are great with pitta or flatbreads and some natural yogurt on the side.

MAKES ABOUT 16

400g can chickpeas, drained and dried

250g minced lamb

1 heaped teaspoon ground turmeric

1 teaspoon ground cumin

½ teaspoon ground cinnamon

½ teaspoon cayenne pepper

½ small packet (about 15g) of flat leaf parsley, finely chopped

5 tablespoons plain flour

1 lemon, peeled, deseeded and flesh finely chopped

1 onion, minced in a food processor or very finely chopped

100g feta cheese, well dried and finely crumbled

vegetable oil, for frying

Maldon sea salt flakes and freshly ground black pepper

To serve

natural yogurt

pitta bread or flatbread

Put the chickpeas, minced lamb, spices and a generous amount of salt and pepper into a food processor and blitz to a paste. Transfer to a mixing bowl and add the parsley, half the flour, the lemon, onion and feta (ensuring the latter 3 ingredients are as dry as possible) along with a little more seasoning. Then use your hands to work the ingredients together really well until you have an evenly combined paste.

Divide the mixture into approximately 16 portions and pat each portion into a small patty shape. Lightly dust each side with the remaining flour.

Heat a large frying pan over a medium-high heat and drizzle in enough vegetable oil to generously coat the base. Once hot (but not smoking), fry the patties for a couple of minutes on each side until nicely browned, then serve with yogurt and pitta or flatbread.

Serve with Aegean Giant Couscous Salad (see page 10) or My Platter of Dreams (see page 21).

Ras el Hanout Sticky Spatchcock Poussin,

I am constantly raiding my store cupboards to bolster flavour in things I cook. This recipe uses that wonderfully aromatic and intense spice blend ras el hanout, along with quince paste or jelly (either is suitable) or apricot jam to give a gratifyingly sticky finish. Now, the only thing you really might find difficult is to decide whether to be sensible and have just half a poussin each or to go the whole hog (or bird!) and enjoy a whole one to yourself.

SERVES 2–4

2 whole poussins

olive oil

2 teaspoons ras el hanout

2 tablespoons quince paste or jelly or apricot jam

Maldon sea salt flakes

Preheat the oven to 220°C (200°C fan), Gas Mark 7. Line a baking tray with baking paper.

To spatchcock each poussin, place it breast-side down on a chopping board. Using a good sturdy pair of kitchen scissors, cut down either side of the backbone and then remove the bone. Turn the poussin over breast-side up and gently press down on it with both hands to flatten as best you can.

Place the poussins, spaced out, on the lined tray. Drizzle each generously with olive oil and sprinkle with the ras el hanout, then use your hands to rub the oil and spice mix all over the top of each poussin. Season generously with salt and roast for 30 minutes.

Remove from the oven, brush the quince jelly or apricot jam over the top of the poussins and roast for a further 10 minutes until cooked through. Remove from the oven, cover loosely with a piece of foil and leave the birds to rest for 10 minutes.

Serve with Spice-roasted Butternut & Black Rice Salad (see page 30) or Cheat's Zereshk Polow (see page 195).

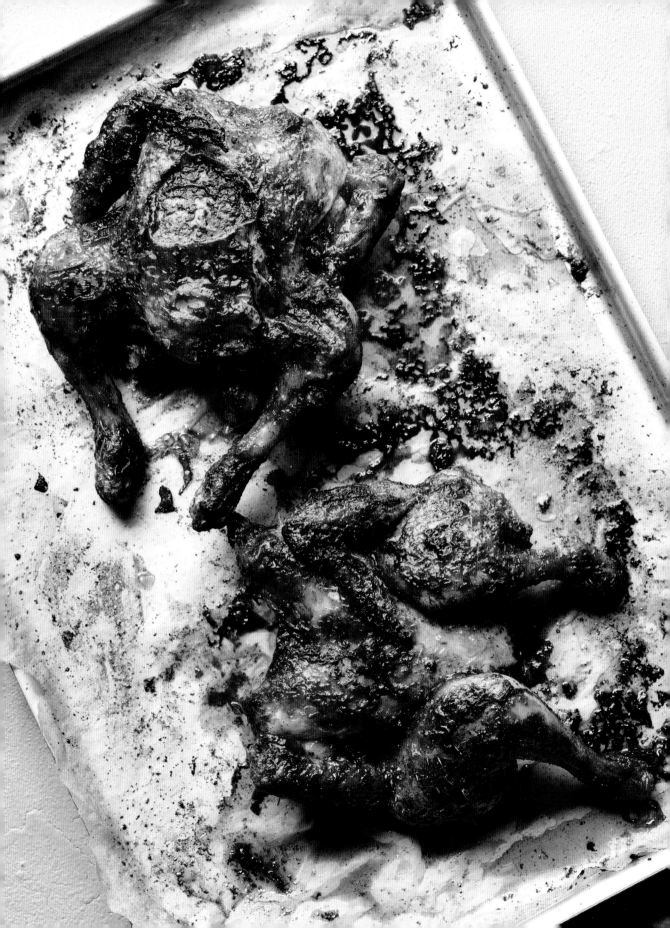

Taas Kabab

I know what you're thinking: you see the word 'kabab' and you're expecting photos of a kebab, right? Well *taas kabab* is something entirely different. It is a Persian recipe of Turkish descent, which we have adapted and make by layering meat and vegetables to create a very flavourful and comforting meal. Every Persian household may argue (as they often do) that their version is different, but this is the recipe I know from my childhood watching my grandmother's sister build the layers before slow-cooking this dish. I guess it is essentially what we in the West call a hotpot and therefore not so unfamiliar after all. It's very subtly spiced and really very delicious, and a hearty recommendation for the colder months.

SERVES 6–8

vegetable oil

2 large onions, roughly chopped

1 large head of garlic, cloves separated, peeled and kept whole

800g lamb neck fillets, cut into 1.5cm-thick chunks

2 teaspoons ground turmeric

½ teaspoon ground cinnamon

5 tablespoons tomato purée

5 carrots, peeled and cut into 3cm chunks

500g new potatoes, cut into 1.5cm-thick slices (halved if small or cut into 3 slices if larger)

6 large tomatoes, halved horizontally

about 250ml water

Maldon sea salt flakes and freshly ground pepper

Greek-style yogurt, to serve

Place a large saucepan with a lid over a medium heat, drizzle in enough vegetable oil to coat the base and fry the onions until softened and translucent. Stir in the garlic cloves. Add the lamb, spices, tomato purée and a generous amount of salt and pepper and mix to coat the lamb well, then cook for 10–15 minutes, stirring occasionally.

Arrange the carrots in a layer over the lamb mixture, then the potatoes, adding a little extra seasoning to the potato layer, and finally top with the tomatoes. Pour over the water, then place the lid on the pan and cook for 30 minutes over a gentle heat without stirring.

Remove the lid and, without stirring, gently shake the pan a little and ensure it has some liquid still left in it. Replace the lid and continue cooking the stew gently, reducing the heat further if necessary, for a further 1½ hours. Carefully remove the ingredients from the pan to serve, with yogurt on the side. This needs no accompaniment, but you can always serve it with bread or steamed basmati rice.

Butterflied Lamb with Tahini Garlic Yogurt

Lamb is my favourite meat of all time: tender, juicy and ever so versatile. But while I love the gentle, slow-cooked, pull-apart approach for cooking a joint, I don't always have the time, so I choose a butterflied leg of lamb for the ultimate quick-cook convenience. How you serve this beauty is up to you. Sometimes I want it with roast potatoes and other times with rice, bulgur wheat or couscous, but I can easily be persuaded to slice it as thinly as possible and pile it into pitta breads with sliced onions, tomatoes and pickles, too.

SERVES 4–6

1–1.5kg butterflied leg of lamb

3 tablespoons natural yogurt

3 fat garlic cloves, minced

2 teaspoons paprika

2 teaspoons ground cumin

2 teaspoons ground coriander

1 teaspoon ground cinnamon

juice of ½ lemon

2 tablespoons olive oil, plus extra for frying

Maldon sea salt flakes and freshly ground black pepper

For the tahini garlic yogurt

150g Greek yogurt

6 tablespoons tahini

1 garlic clove, minced

good squeeze of lemon juice

To serve

4–6 tomatoes, quartered

sliced red onion

flatbreads

Remove the lamb from the refrigerator 20 minutes before you intend to marinate it and ensure it is splayed open and as flat as possible so that the meat cooks evenly. If there are any sides with much thicker meat, use a small sharp knife to make incisions to open them up and flatten as evenly as possible.

For the marinade, mix all the remaining ingredients together in a large mixing bowl, seasoning generously with salt and pepper. Place the lamb on an oven tray and rub the marinade all over, really working it in. Cover with clingfilm and marinate for a minimum of 30 minutes at room temperature, or overnight in the refrigerator if preferred. Remove from the refrigerator 30 minutes or so before cooking to come up to room temperature.

Preheat the oven to 220°C (200°C fan), Gas Mark 7. Line a baking tray with baking paper.

continued overleaf

Place a large frying pan over a medium heat, drizzle in a little olive oil, and once hot, add the marinated lamb to the pan, skin-side down. Seal the lamb until browned on all sides, without letting it blacken or burn. It should have a nice crust in about 10 minutes.

Transfer the lamb to the lined tray and roast for 20–25 minutes, depending on how you like your meat cooked. I like it very pink and juicy, but if you prefer medium or well done, leave it in for a further 5–10 minutes. Once the meat is cooked to your liking, remove from the oven and leave to rest covered with foil for 10–15 minutes.

Meanwhile, mix the tahini garlic yogurt ingredients together in a bowl and season with salt and pepper, then thin down with some lukewarm water to a sauce consistency.

Serve the lamb thinly sliced with the tahini garlic yogurt, tomatoes, sliced onion and flatbreads.

Serve with Spice-roasted Butternut & Black Rice Salad (see page 30), Layered Vegetable & Feta Bake (see page 138), Ras el Hanout & Sweet Potato with Tahini Yogurt & Herb Oil (see page 165) or Spice-roasted Potatoes with Tomato, Pepper & Harissa Sauce (see page 166).

Tahchin Two Ways

I shared the most classic tahchin recipe using chicken and barberries with you in my book *Simply*, but I'm delighted to say that there are more versions. Among the most popular are the minced meat tahchin or the aubergine tahchin. Both are delicious; however, I lean towards the meat filling because I do love my meat and the family loves it, too. Having said that, the aubergine filling is a satisfying vegetarian alternative.

SERVES 4–6

500g basmati rice

300g Greek yogurt

3 large eggs

1g (about a pinch) saffron threads, ground to a powder using a pestle and mortar, then steeped in 5 tablespoons boiling water until cool

50g butter, melted

melted ghee or vegetable oil, for greasing

Maldon sea salt flakes and freshly ground black pepper

For the aubergine filling (VEGETARIAN)

3 large aubergines, peeled and cut into 2.5cm cubes

olive oil

1 teaspoon ground cumin

½ teaspoon ground cinnamon

For the meat filling

vegetable oil

1 large onion, finely chopped

500g minced lamb

1 teaspoon garlic granules

1 teaspoon ground turmeric

½ teaspoon ground cinnamon

2 tablespoons tomato purée

50g butter

4 generous handfuls of frozen peas, rinsed in cold water to defrost and drained

To prepare the aubergine filling

Preheat the oven to 200°C (180°C fan), Gas Mark 6. Line a large baking tray with baking paper.

Place the aubergine cubes on the lined tray, drizzle generously with olive oil and rub in. Season very generously with salt and pepper and the cumin and cinnamon, then use your hands to coat the cubes evenly in the seasoning and spices. Spread out in a single layer and roast for 25 minutes until nicely browned and cooked through. Remove from the oven and set aside.

continued overleaf

To prepare the meat filling

Place a large saucepan over a high heat, drizzle in some vegetable oil and stir-fry the onion until translucent and beginning to turn golden around the edges. Add the minced lamb and immediately break it up as finely as you can to prevent it cooking in clumps. Add the garlic granules, spices and tomato purée and stir through to coat the meat and until cooked. Add the butter and a very generous amount of salt and pepper, followed by the peas, then stir until the butter has melted and everything is evenly combined. Taste and adjust the seasoning if desired, then set aside.

To assemble

Bring a large saucepan of water to the boil. Add the rice and stir to avoid the grains from sticking together, then parboil for about 6–7 minutes until the grains turn from a dullish off-white colour to a more opaque, brilliant white and have slightly elongated – they should still remain firm to the bite. Drain and immediately rinse thoroughly under cold running water, running your fingers through the rice, until all the grains are well rinsed of starch and completely cooled. Drain the rice thoroughly by shaking the sieve well, then leave for any remaining water to drain for 10 minutes. Shake off any excess water before use.

Put the yogurt, eggs, saffron solution and a generous amount of salt and pepper (bearing in mind that you will need more than you think, as the rice will increase in volume and require more seasoning) into a large mixing bowl and stir until evenly combined. Stir in the parboiled rice, then the melted butter and mix well.

Preheat the oven to 200°C (180°C fan), Gas Mark 6. Line the base of a 32 x 22cm ovenproof dish with baking paper and brush the paper and sides with melted ghee or vegetable oil (if using a nonstick dish, you can omit the paper and just brush with melted ghee or vegetable oil).

Pour half the rice mixture into the dish and spread it out. Add your chosen filling on top in an even layer, then cover with the remaining rice mixture and smooth the surface. Bake on the lowest shelf in the oven for 1 hour 20–30 minutes, or until the edges are browned.

Once cooked, place a tray or large heatproof platter over the dish and carefully flip the tahchin on to the tray or platter and cut into squares to serve.

Serve the aubergine tahchin with Burnt Courgettes with Lemon & Feta Yogurt (see page 145); serve the meat tahchin with Mama Ghanoush (see page 158).

Tavuk Güveç

My love for Turkish cuisine is well known and this chicken recipe is another one of those recipes that just has to be shared. Having published the meat version of *güveç* in my previous book *Persiana Everyday*, I wanted to present this lighter chicken version to you, too. The Turkish pepper paste of the classic recipe can be hard to find, so I have replaced it here with paprika. But should you find a jar, simply swap it in for the paprika to experience the real deal. Either way, this is another one-pot comfort classic that is so delicious it will become a household favourite. I like to serve this with plain boiled rice or bread.

SERVES 6

olive oil

2 large onions, roughly chopped

1kg bone-in, skinless chicken thighs

1 head of garlic, cloves separated, peeled and kept whole

4 bay leaves

1 teaspoon paprika

1 teaspoon pul biber chilli flakes

1 teaspoon dried wild oregano

1 teaspoon dried mint

4 tablespoons tomato purée

500g new potatoes, halved

2 red peppers, cored, deseeded and cut into big chunks

4 large tomatoes, halved

Maldon sea salt flakes and freshly ground black pepper

Place a large saucepan over a medium-high heat, drizzle in some olive oil and cook the onions until softened and translucent. Stir in the chicken and garlic cloves, then add the bay leaves, spices, dried herbs, tomato purée and a generous amount of salt and pepper. Cook for 5 minutes, stirring occasionally. Add the potatoes, red peppers and tomatoes and cook for a further 5 minutes.

Pour over enough boiling water to just about cover the ingredients, reduce the heat to a gentle medium heat and cook uncovered for 2 hours, stirring occasionally. Taste and adjust the seasoning if desired, then serve. This needs no accompaniment.

The Kids' Chicken Korma

This is one of my kids' favourite dishes I like to cook at home, but don't for a second think that this recipe is just for kids – this is simply a family favourite. 'Korma' comes from a Persian term *ghormeh*, meaning 'stew', and although this particular recipe bears no resemblance to anything Persian, Indian cuisine has so much influence from Persia. To make it a little more grown up, add ½–1 teaspoon chilli flakes. Kids generally prefer chicken breast meat, but I prefer chicken thighs, so if that's your preference too, substitute 800g boneless, skinless thigh fillets and cook for 1½ hours instead.

SERVES 4–6

2–3 tablespoons vegetable oil or ghee

2 large onions, finely chopped

650g boneless, skinless chicken
   breasts, split lengthways and cut
   into 5mm-thick slices

2 teaspoons medium curry powder

1 heaped teaspoon ground turmeric

50g desiccated coconut

50g ground almonds

2 tablespoons caster sugar

400ml can coconut milk

Maldon sea salt flakes and freshly
   ground black pepper

steamed basmati rice, to serve

Heat a medium-sized saucepan over a medium heat, add the vegetable oil or ghee and fry the onions until soft and translucent, but do not let them brown. Add the chicken, spices, coconut and ground almonds and mix well until evenly combined. Add a generous amount of salt and pepper and then add the sugar and cook the mixture for 5–6 minutes, stirring regularly to prevent any browning or burning.

Pour in the coconut milk and stir until evenly combined – the liquid should mostly cover the chicken. Allow the chicken to simmer gently, uncovered, for about an hour or so until tender and the sauce is thick enough to coat the back of a spoon. Serve with steamed basmati rice.

Pan-fried Salmon, with Barberry Butter

People always ask me how else they can use barberries at home, and although I have literally dozens of suggestions, one of the most common answers I give is to make a butter compound out of them along with any herbs and flavours you like – then use that butter with everything. The lovely citrusy character of barberries means that you can essentially treat them as you would when adding lemon to a dish, but without the bitterness or liquid. Here, they provide a wonderful berry sharpness that works so well with the fatty salmon that it really is a perfect pairing.

SERVES 2–4

olive oil

4 skinless salmon fillets,
  125–150g each

Maldon sea salt flakes and freshly
  ground black pepper

For the barberry butter

75g butter, softened

2 tablespoons dried barberries,
  finely chopped

1 teaspoon pul biber chilli flakes

1 teaspoon garlic granules

1 tablespoon clear honey

Put all the barberry butter ingredients into a small bowl, add a good seasoning of salt and pepper and mix together well. You can use the butter straight away or wrap in baking paper and refrigerate for later use.

Heat a large frying pan over a medium-high heat and drizzle in a little olive oil. Season the salmon fillets on the top side with salt and pepper, then add, top-side down, to the pan. Cook for a couple of minutes, then carefully turn over and immediately add the butter. As soon as the butter melts, begin basting the salmon fillets quickly and repeatedly to prevent the butter from burning, for 2 minutes, or until just cooked through. Serve immediately, with the butter spooned over.

Serve with Nectarine, Halloumi & Cucumber Salad with Cashews (see page 25) or Warm Orzo, Black-eyed Bean & Herb Salad (see page 42).

Spiced & Soupy Seafood Rice

I absolutely love comforting recipes like this for the colder months, especially when seafood is concerned. Admittedly, seafood often feels like a summer thing, but this is really the kind of hearty dish I want to eat when the weather is cold and I need a little warming burst of sunshine to brighten up the darker days. And yes – don't even give it two minutes' thought – serve some crusty bread on the side. It may not be needed, but I feel my whole being benefits from the frequent enjoyment of double carbs, and yours might, too!

SERVES 4–6

olive oil

1 large onion, finely chopped

1 large head of garlic, cloves separated, bashed, peeled and kept whole

1 bay leaf

2 tablespoons harissa

1 tablespoon dried wild oregano

2 large tomatoes, cored and roughly diced

1 large yellow pepper, cored, deseeded and diced

400g can chopped tomatoes

1 teaspoon caster sugar

1.5 litres cold water

200g arborio or carnaroli risotto rice

1kg fresh mussels, cleaned

250g fresh or frozen raw peeled tiger prawns, defrosted if frozen

75g butter, roughly chopped

½ small packet (about 15g) of flat leaf parsley, roughly chopped, some reserved for garnish

Maldon sea salt flakes and freshly ground black pepper

Place a large saucepan over a medium-high heat, drizzle in some olive oil and cook the onion until softened. Add the garlic cloves and continue cooking until the onion is translucent. Add the bay leaf, harissa, oregano, fresh tomatoes, yellow pepper and a generous amount of salt and pepper and cook, stirring, for a few minutes. Next, add the canned tomatoes and sugar and stir again, then pour in the water and stir. Reduce to a gentle medium heat and simmer, uncovered, for 45 minutes.

Add the rice and stir once, then cook for 15 minutes. Taste and adjust the seasoning if desired. Check the liquid volume and add a little hot water if needed, then stir in the mussels, cover again and cook for 5 minutes until the shells have opened. Stir in the prawns, cover again and cook for another minute. Lastly, add the butter with the parsley and stir until melted. Discard any mussels that have not opened, then taste and adjust the seasoning if desired and serve immediately in shallow bowls and scatter with parsley. This needs no accompaniment other than bread.

Vegetables
& Pulses

Layered Vegetable & Feta Bake

This layered vegetable bake requires little effort and doesn't compromise on flavour – I can't recommend this loaf-tin-baked beauty highly enough. I love the oozy dots of feta in it, and the cheese marries so well with the sauce, too.

SERVES 2–4

1 large aubergine, cut into 5mm-thick slices

1 large courgette, cut into 5mm-thick slices

olive oil

1 large red pepper, cored, deseeded and cut into 6 long strips

2 fat garlic cloves, thinly sliced

½ teaspoon chilli flakes

400g can chopped tomatoes

1 teaspoon caster sugar

200g feta cheese, broken into small chunks (omit for a vegan option)

Maldon sea salt flakes and freshly ground black pepper

Preheat the oven to 200°C (180°C fan), Gas Mark 6. Line a large baking tray with baking paper.

Lay the aubergine and courgette slices on the lined baking tray, brush with olive oil and season well with salt and pepper. Roast for 35–40 minutes. Remove from the oven and transfer the roasted veg to a plate.

Turn your oven up to its highest setting and line the baking tray with fresh baking paper. Lay the red pepper strips, skin-side down, on the lined tray, brush the exposed sides with olive oil and roast for 15 minutes. Remove from the oven and reduce the oven temperature to 220°C (200°C fan), Gas Mark 7.

To make the sauce, place a small saucepan over a medium heat, drizzle in some olive oil and fry the garlic slices until translucent. Add the chilli flakes and stir for a minute before adding the canned tomatoes, sugar and a good seasoning of salt and pepper. Cook for 20 minutes or so on a gentle simmer, then remove from the heat and blitz with a stick blender until nice and smooth. Taste and adjust the seasoning if desired.

Pour half the sauce into a 900g/2lb loaf tin, add a layer of the peppers, arranged widthways or diagonally, then some courgettes and top with enough of the feta to cover the surface and just a little of the sauce. Layer in the remaining vegetables and feta, then cover with the remaining sauce. Carefully press down, then bake for 30 minutes until piping hot. Remove from the oven and leave to rest for 5 minutes, then place a plate over the top, carefully flip on to the plate and serve. Don't worry if it doesn't look neat or collapses – it will still taste sublime.

Serve with Butterflied Lamb with Tahini Garlic Yogurt (see page 123) or Charred Broccoli with Lemons, Chillies, & Yogurt (see page 154).

Bean, Pepper & Thyme Khorak

Khorak is to Persians what a *ragoût* is to the French. Classically it would be a meat braise of some sort, but these days there are many varieties including one with green beans. As a devoted lover of legumes, there isn't a single variety of pulse that I don't love – but rarely do I make them the main dish on a table. This colourful recipe is worthy of centrepiece stardom because it's bright, vibrant, delicious and really easy to make. As a bonus, you can use any beans you like, which means you'll be more likely to make it time and time again. Enjoy on its own or with rice or crusty bread.

SERVES 4–6

150g semi-dried tomatoes in oil, drained and oil reserved

1 large onion, finely chopped

3 large peppers (any colour, but I like red, orange and yellow), cored, deseeded and cut into thin strips

6 garlic cloves, thinly sliced

8–10 fleshy sprigs of thyme or 3 woody sprigs of thyme, or 1 heaped teaspoon dried thyme

400g can cannellini beans, drained and rinsed

400g can red kidney beans, drained and rinsed

400g can chopped tomatoes

1 teaspoon pul biber chilli flakes

Maldon sea salt flakes and freshly ground black pepper

crusty bread, to serve

Place a large, deep frying pan or shallow saucepan over a medium-high heat, drizzle in some of the oil from the semi-dried tomatoes and fry the onion until beginning to brown around the edges. Add the peppers and stir-fry with the onion until they are completely softened and also beginning to brown around the edges.

Next, add the garlic slices, thyme (discarding any woody stalks), cannellini beans, kidney beans, canned tomatoes, pul biber and a very generous amount of salt and pepper, stir well and cook over a medium-high heat for 15–20 minutes, stirring occasionally to prevent sticking. Lastly, add the semi-dried tomatoes, taste and adjust the seasoning if desired, then cook for a further 10–15 minutes before serving with crusty bread.

Serve with Cabbage 'Bowl' Dolma (see page 147) or Traybaked Spicy Chickpeas & Aubergines with Yogurt & Herbs (see page 174).

Smoked Aubergine with Lime & Maple Dressing

This is a wonderful way to enjoy aubergines with less traditional flavours than the usual Middle Eastern offering. Even my ordinarily aubergine-shy husband ate more than his fair share of this, making me determined to let you in on the recipe by including it in a book one day . . . and so here we are. I hope you love it.

SERVES 2–4

2 large aubergines

4 springs onions, thinly sliced diagonally from root to tip

½ small packet (about 15g) of fresh coriander, finely chopped

½ teaspoon pul biber chilli flakes, or more to taste

generous handful of salted peanuts, roughly chopped

For the dressing

2 tablespoons olive oil

1 heaped tablespoon maple syrup

finely grated zest and juice of 1 fat unwaxed lime

Maldon sea salt flakes and freshly ground black pepper

Smoke the aubergines whole over an open flame either on a barbecue or over a gas hob, using tongs to turn them, until the skin has crackled and become ashen all over, the aubergines have collapsed by half and the flesh is completely soft on the inside. Remove from the heat and allow the aubergines to cool until you can handle them.

Mix the dressing ingredients together with a generous seasoning of salt and pepper in a jug or small bowl.

Holding the stalk end, make an incision down one side of each aubergine without cutting all the way through and open out the aubergine to reveal the flesh inside. Gently shake off any excess liquid or pat it off with kitchen paper. Divide the dressing between the aubergines and very gently mash it into the flesh a little with a fork. Sprinkle over the spring onions, coriander and pul biber, top with the peanuts and serve.

Serve with Aegean Giant Couscous Salad (see page 10) or Pan-fried Salmon with Barberry Butter (see page 133).

Burnt Courgettes with Lemon & Feta Yogurt

Courgettes really do get a bad rap sometimes, but they are a firm favourite of mine and my preferred method to cook them is always roasting them in the oven. Here, the charring really gives them an added depth and dimension that works beautifully with yogurt and feta, and the spike of lemon and mint freshens this beauty of a recipe so well. Perfect for dipping toasted bread into, or eating on the side of roasted meats like lamb and chicken.

SERVES 4–6

4 courgettes, halved lengthways and cut into 3cm chunks

olive oil

500g thick Greek yogurt

200g feta cheese, broken into small chunks

3 spring onions, thinly sliced

1 fat garlic clove, minced

finely grated zest of 1 unwaxed lemon

1 small packet (about 30g) of mint, leaves picked, rolled up tightly and thinly sliced into ribbons, reserving some for garnish

2 teaspoons dried wild oregano, reserving some for garnish

Maldon sea salt flakes and freshly ground black pepper

toasted pitta, to serve

Preheat your oven to its highest setting. Line a large baking tray with baking paper.

Spread the courgette chunks out on the lined tray, drizzle with olive oil and roast for 18–20 minutes until deeply charred in parts. Remove from the oven and leave to cool.

Put all the remaining ingredients into a mixing bowl, add a drizzle of olive oil and season well with salt and pepper, then mix everything together.

Once the courgettes have cooled, give them a rough chop, then add them to the yogurt mixture and stir together. Drizzle with olive oil scatter over more mint and oregano, and serve with toasted pitta.

Serve with Root Vegetable, Chickpea, Feta & Barberry Tart (see page 149) or Cabbage 'Bowl' Dolma (see page 147).

Cabbage 'Bowl' Dolma

When I was a kid, onion and cabbage dolmas were always my favourite – they would absorb the poaching liquid and sweeten it in a way that vine leaves didn't quite do. Although 'bowl' dolma (using a small bowl to help form the dolma) is not a classic recipe, anything that makes my life easier is welcome in my repertoire. While Persians like meat in their classic dolma, I've made these vegan to suit everyone as either a main course or an accompaniment to meat or fish. Note that dolmas ALWAYS taste better made a day ahead.

SERVES 4–6

1 large head of Savoy cabbage, leaves separated

olive oil

1 large onion, finely chopped

4 heaped tablespoons tomato purée

2 teaspoons garlic granules

1 teaspoon paprika

1 teaspoon ground cumin

1 teaspoon pul biber chilli flakes

½ teaspoon ground cinnamon

250g basmati rice

1 small packet (about 30g) of flat leaf parsley, finely chopped

1 small packet (about 30g) of chives, thinly sliced

1 small packet (about 30g) of fresh coriander, finely chopped

1 small packet (about 30g) of dill, finely chopped

Maldon sea salt flakes and freshly ground black pepper

For the tomato sauce

400g can chopped tomatoes

2 teaspoons caster sugar

good squeeze of lemon juice

For the poaching liquid

600ml boiling water

2 vegetable or vegan stock cubes

2 tablespoons tomato purée

2 tablespoons caster sugar

To make the tomato sauce, place a small saucepan over a gentle medium heat, add the ingredients along with a generous amount of salt and pepper and bring to a gentle boil. Cook for 20 minutes, stirring regularly, until reduced to a thick sauce-like consistency. Remove from the heat and leave to cool. Using a stick blender, blitz the sauce until smooth.

continued overleaf

Bring a large saucepan of water to the boil, add the cabbage leaves and boil for about 10 minutes or so until tender and flexible. Drain and cover with cold water to cool them down.

Preheat the oven to 200°C (180°C fan), Gas Mark 6. Select a medium-large ovenproof dish.

Place a frying pan over a medium-high heat, drizzle in some olive oil and fry the onion until softened but not coloured. Add the tomato purée, garlic granules, spices and a generous seasoning of salt and pepper and cook the spice mixture for 2–3 minutes, stirring regularly. Add the rice and quickly stir to coat in the mixture, then add the herbs, mix well again and remove from the heat but continue to mix until everything is evenly combined. Set aside.

Drain the cabbage leaves and pat dry. Choose the largest leaves and cut out and discard the stems. Line the bottom of a very small bowl, about 10cm or so in diameter, with a cabbage leaf. Divide the rice mixture into 8–10 portions, depending on how many large leaves you get from the cabbage (you can also overlay smaller and broken leaves), then place a portion on the leaf in the bowl and wrap the leaf around the filling to enclose. Carefully remove the dolma from the bowl. Repeat with the remaining cabbage leaves and rice mixture.

Select a deep ovenproof dish or baking tin that will fit all the dolma snugly. Drizzle olive oil in the bottom of the dish and line it with any remaining leaves. Carefully transfer all the dolma into the dish.

Stir the poaching liquid ingredients together until the stock cubes have dissolved, then pour into the dish – the liquid level should be high enough to cook the rice. Pour the tomato sauce over the dolma, then cover the dish with a double layer of foil and bake in the lowest part of the oven for an hour. Lower the oven temperature to 180°C (160°C fan), Gas Mark 4 then bake for a further 30 minutes. Remove from the oven and leave to cool. These are best made the day before eating to allow the flavours to intensify, so refrigerate them until you are ready to serve the next day.

To reheat, preheat the oven to 200°C (180°C fan), Gas Mark 6. Place the dolma in an ovenproof dish, add a splash of water, then cover with foil. Reheat for 20–25 minutes, or until warmed through. These are best eaten warm rather than piping hot.

Serve with Butterflied Lamb with Tahini Garlic Yogurt (see page 123) or Burnt Courgettes with Lemon & Feta Yogurt (see page 145).

Root Vegetable, Chickpea, Feta & Barberry Tart

I first created this recipe for a cookery class in the run-up to Christmas when I wanted to give students a wonderful vegetarian dish that would be perfect as a main course for the festive table. Fast forward many years later and it's simply a wonderful dish to serve at any time, but its use of root vegetables lends itself particularly well to the autumn and winter months. It is so incredibly forgiving because, no matter how you make it, it will look beautiful and therefore makes a worthy centrepiece whatever the season. What's more, it's substantial and delicious.

SERVES 4–6

about 2 tablespoons vegetable oil

1 large onion, finely chopped

2 fat garlic cloves, finely chopped

pinch of saffron threads, finely crumbled or ground using a pestle and mortar

2 parsnips, peeled and coarsely grated

300g celeriac, peeled and coarsely grated

400g can chickpeas, drained

1 teaspoon sumac

1 heaped teaspoon ground coriander

1 teaspoon ground cinnamon

1 teaspoon pul biber chilli flakes

2 large carrots, peeled and coarsely grated

finely grated zest of 1 unwaxed lemon and juice of ½

1 heaped tablespoon clear honey, plus extra for drizzling

1 small packet (about 30g) of dill, finely chopped

1 small packet (about 30g) of flat leaf parsley, finely chopped

2 good handfuls of dried barberries

200g feta cheese, finely crumbled

100g pistachio nuts, roughly chopped

6 sheets of filo pastry (each about 480 x 250mm)

75g butter, melted

Maldon sea salt flakes and freshly ground black pepper

Preheat the oven to 220°C (200°C fan), Gas Mark 7. Select a 26cm round ovenproof dish.

Place a large frying pan over a medium heat, add the vegetable oil and fry the onion until soft but not coloured too much. Add the garlic and cook, stirring well, for a couple of minutes.

continued overleaf

Stir the saffron through the onion mixture and then add the parsnips and celeriac first, stirring for a couple of minutes, before mixing in the chickpeas and spices. Then add the carrots and a generous amount of salt and pepper. Remove the pan from the heat, add the lemon zest and juice, honey, herbs and barberries and mix until combined, then carefully fold in the feta and pistachios.

Lay 3 filo pastry sheets in the base of the ovenproof dish at different angles with enough overhanging the edges of the dish to cover the top of the tart, but ensuring the base is completely covered. Brush generously with melted butter and then tip in the root vegetable mixture and compress to fill the dish. Scrunch the edges of the loose pastry around the sides of the tart to make a ruffled edge, like a kind of crust. Brush the exposed edges with butter. Scrunch up the remaining filo pastry sheets loosely on top to cover the surface and then brush with the remaining butter. Bake for 25–30 minutes until nicely golden brown.

Remove from the oven, leave to cool for a few minutes and then serve with a generous drizzle of honey on top if desired.

Serve with Mama Ghanoush (see page 158).

Cabbage with Tamarind, Maple & Black Pepper Butter

It's fair to say that I eat a lot of cabbage of every description. I use it in different ways, from raw to cooked, from dolmas to pastas and stir-fries – nothing is exempt from improvement with a little added cabbage. This recipe contains a method I absolutely love to use when cooking cabbage. The butter really takes the cabbage to another level and makes this humble brassica something altogether very special and unique.

SERVES 2–4

olive oil

1 large head of sweetheart cabbage,
   stalk left on, quartered

100ml cold water

50g butter

1 heaped tablespoon tamarind paste

2 tablespoons maple syrup

1 teaspoon coarse freshly ground
   black pepper

Maldon sea salt flakes

Place a large frying pan over a medium heat and drizzle in some olive oil. Arrange the cabbage wedges in the pan, sitting on one cut side and with the stalk ends in the centre of the pan, and fry for 5 minutes. Pour in the cold water, increase the heat a little and cover the pan with a lid, then cook for about 6–7 minutes until the water has evaporated.

Remove the lid and turn the cabbage wedges to cook on the other cut side for 3–4 minutes, uncovered, then add the butter. Mix the tamarind, maple syrup and pepper together, then add to the pan with a good seasoning of salt and stir it into the melted butter quickly – a little charring is good, but take care to avoid it from burning. Baste the cabbage as best you can, then flip back on to the other side and keep basting for a few more minutes. Serve with any remaining flavoured butter from the pan drizzled over.

Serve with Pan-fried Salmon with Barberry Butter (see page 133).

Charred Broccoli with Lemons, Chillies & Yogurt

Broccoli is one green vegetable that everyone in our house likes, and since I've become a step-parent, I've realized this may be as good as it gets – so I am constantly making things with broccoli to ensure some vegetables other than potatoes are being consumed. Truth is, I absolutely love the stuff myself, whether the classic large florets or the Tenderstem variety, so I do like to add it to many dishes for flavour and texture. While I enjoy it simply with salt and pepper, sometimes a change is needed and a few big flavour items are required to give things a little lift. Sour, spicy, tangy and delicious, this dish is a fantastic way to keep broccoli on the menu.

SERVES 3–4

1 large head or 2 small heads of broccoli

olive oil

100g Greek-style yogurt or plant-based-yogurt, thinned down with water to the pouring consistency of double cream

3 pickled red chillies, thinly sliced

1–2 preserved lemons (or to taste), deseeded and finely chopped

1 teaspoon nigella seeds

Maldon sea salt flakes and freshly ground black pepper

Break the broccoli into florets, then peel the large central stalk with a vegetable peeler and slice into discs. Put all the florets and stalk pieces into a large heatproof bowl and pour over enough boiling water to cover them, ensuring they are all submerged. Leave to blanch for 5 minutes, then drain into a colander and leave to sit.

Heat a griddle pan over a high heat, and once hot, return the broccoli to the bowl, drizzle generously with olive oil and turn to coat, then char the broccoli for a few minutes on both sides until it bears char marks. Remove from the pan and place on a platter, then season well with pepper and just a little salt. Drizzle with the loosened yogurt, sprinkle over the pickled chillies, preserved lemons and nigella seeds, then serve.

Serve with Layered Vegetable & Feta Bake (see page 138) or Ras el Hanout & Orange Lamb Cutlet Platter (see page 109).

Bhaji Buns

I love an onion bhaji and this is my homage to them, using store cupboard spices. I have paired this with a soft white roll, and taken inspiration from chaat street food where treats are laden with yogurt, tamarind sauce, herbs and sev – a crispy fine noodle – but to make it easier for you, I've used cornflakes to add crunch.

MAKES 4

2 large onions, finely chopped

6 tablespoons gram flour

1 teaspoon baking powder

2 teaspoons ground turmeric

1 teaspoon pul biber chilli flakes

1 teaspoon cumin seeds

1 teaspoon garlic granules

juice of ½ lemon

½ small packet (about 15g) of fresh coriander, finely chopped, plus extra leaves for garnish

vegetable oil, for frying

Maldon sea salt flakes and freshly ground black pepper

To serve

4 soft white rolls

sweet tamarind sauce or mango chutney

Greek-style yogurt or plant-based yogurt

pomegranate seeds

handful of unsweetened cornflakes or plain crisps

Put the onions into a mixing bowl with a generous amount of salt (this will encourage moisture to be released, which helps bind the mixture) and stir very well with a fork, then leave to sit for 10 minutes.

Stir the onions again, add all the remaining ingredients, except the oil, with a good seasoning of black pepper and mix everything together until you have a cohesive batter. Leave the batter to sit for 10 minutes.

Meanwhile, heat a large frying pan over a medium-high heat, pour in about 2.5cm vegetable oil and bring to frying temperature (add a pinch of the mixture: if it sizzles immediately, the oil is hot enough). Line a large plate with a double layer of kitchen paper.

Stir the onion mixture once more, then use your hands to form 4 round patties (the mix will be wet, but don't worry, just shape them as best you can), then flatten them. Fry the patties 1 or 2 at a time, depending on how many you can fit in your pan, for about 4–5 minutes or so until deep brown on the underside, then flipping over gently using a slotted spoon and fork until deep brown all over. Remove with the slotted spoon and transfer to the paper-lined plate to drain. Serve in soft white rolls, and top with tamarind sauce or mango chutney, yogurt, pomegranate seeds, coriander leaves and cornflakes or plain crisps. This needs no accompaniment.

Mama Ghanoush

It would be fair to say that Mama Ghanoush is not actually an authentic Middle Eastern recipe, so I would like you to think of her as baba's spicy other half. With all the joys of a classic baba ghanoush, and a few additions including pul biber, yogurt and fresh herbs to give it a little lift, try this when you feel like having something with a more complex and punchy flavour.

SERVES 4–6

4 large aubergines

2 fat garlic cloves, crushed or minced

½ small packet (about 15g) of fresh coriander, finely chopped, some reserved for garnish

½ small packet (about 15g) of flat leaf parsley, finely chopped, some reserved for garnish

1 heaped teaspoon pul biber chilli flakes, plus extra for garnish

150g Greek yogurt or plant-based yogurt

5 tablespoons tahini

finely grated zest and juice of 1 fat unwaxed lemon

olive oil

Maldon sea salt flakes and freshly ground black pepper

toasted mini pitta, to serve

Smoke the aubergines whole over an open flame either on a barbecue or over a gas hob, using tongs to turn them, until the skin has crackled and become ashen all over, the aubergines have collapsed by half and the flesh is completely soft on the inside. Remove from the heat and allow the aubergines to cool until you can handle them.

Holding the stalk end, make an incision down one side of each aubergine without cutting all the way through and open out the aubergines to reveal the flesh inside. Scoop out the flesh into a sieve and strain off any excess liquid, and discard the skins.

Put the aubergine flesh and all the remaining ingredients into a mixing bowl with a good drizzle of olive oil and a generous seasoning of salt and pepper and mix well. Taste and adjust the seasoning if desired.

To serve, spread thinly over a large plate, drizzle more olive oil on top and scatter over the reserved herbs and pul biber. Serve with toasted mini pitta.

Serve with Nargessi Kofta Loaf (see page 107), or Butterflied Lamb with Tahini Garlic Yogurt (see page 123) or Afghani Polow (see page 191).

Nimroo Mirzai

This is my own creation based on the popular Persian dish, *mirza ghasemi* (which you can find the recipe for in my book *Persiana*), using smoked aubergines, tomatoes and eggs, and finished with walnuts. It has all the joys of the former but in a breakfast dish that scrambles eggs the way Persians do to make a classic *nimroo tomat* (egg and tomato scramble). The addition of garlic, cooked in a sweet, mellow way along with the tomato and turmeric, feels like it shouldn't work . . . but it does! Perfect on thick white or sourdough toast, it's incredibly good at any time of day.

SERVES 4

olive oil

4 garlic cloves, finely chopped

1 teaspoon ground turmeric

2 tablespoons tomato purée

2 large tomatoes, cut into 8

4 eggs

generous knob of butter

Maldon sea salt flakes and freshly
   ground black pepper

toasted bread or flatbread, to serve

Place a frying pan over a medium heat and drizzle in a little olive oil, then add the garlic and stir for a minute or so until it begins to cook without any colour.

Add the turmeric, tomato purée and a generous amount of pepper and some salt, mix together and cook, stirring, for a couple of minutes. Add the fresh tomatoes and stir again (this should all be sizzling but not burning), then cover the pan with a lid and cook for 6–7 minutes until the tomatoes are cooked through, stirring occasionally to ensure it doesn't burn.

Stir well and then increase the heat just a little. Crack the eggs into the pan, add the butter and begin scrambling the eggs into the mixture. The texture should be wet and loose so don't expect it to look like scrambled eggs, just keep stirring until the eggs are cooked, then serve with toasted bread or flatbread. This needs no accompaniment.

Marinated Halloumi Skewers

Whether you call it halloumi or hellim, it is the one ingredient that I always have in my refrigerator for when you need rescuing and you have nothing else. These skewers are Mediterranean in essence, but with a little spice to boot. My favourite way to eat them is to place the skewer on to some flatbread and slide the ingredients off, then drizzle with a little honey (trust me on this), add a squeeze of lemon juice and a little chilli sauce, roll it up and tuck in. If you don't have skewers, simply roast the ingredients on a baking tray.

MAKES 3

250g block of halloumi cheese, cut into 6 cubes

½ red pepper, cored, deseeded and cut into 6 pieces

½ yellow pepper, cored, deseeded and cut into 6 pieces

6 cherry tomatoes, halved

1 teaspoon dried mint

1 teaspoon dried wild oregano

1 teaspoon ground coriander

1 teaspoon paprika

3 tablespoons garlic oil

freshly ground black pepper

To serve

3 flatbreads

chilli sauce of your choice

lemon wedges

honey, for drizzling (optional)

Preheat your oven to its highest setting. Line a baking tray with baking paper.

Put the halloumi, peppers and tomatoes into a mixing bowl, add the dried herbs, spices, garlic oil and a generous amount of black pepper and gently mix together to evenly coat the ingredients in the oil and seasonings.

Divide the ingredients into 3 equal portions and push each portion on to a wooden or metal skewer. Place the skewers on the lined tray and roast for 15–16 minutes until cooked. You can also cook them on a barbecue, turning frequently (if using wooden skewers, presoak them in cold water for about 30 minutes). Serve with flatbreads, your favourite chilli sauce, lemon wedges for squeezing over and a drizzle of honey if desired.

Serve with Cauliflower & Lentil Salad (see page 17) or Warm Orzo, Black-eyed Bean & Herb Salad (see page 42).

Ras el Hanout & Sweet Potato with Tahini Yogurt & Herb Oil

Sweet potatoes are wonderfully versatile and their natural sweetness makes them a perfect match for spices and other aromatic flavours. You can rely on the ras el hanout spice blend to do most of the work here – just roast the sweet potatoes, add a simple tahini yogurt and serve with a quick herb oil, pine nuts and pomegranate seeds.

SERVES 4–6

4 sweet potatoes, peeled and cut into 1.5cm-thick discs

4 tablespoons olive oil

2 heaped tablespoons ras el hanout

2 tablespoons pine nuts

good handful of pomegranate seeds

Maldon sea salt flakes and freshly ground black pepper

For the herb oil

½ small packet (about 15g) of flat leaf parsley

½ small packet (about 15g) of dill

½ small packet (about 15g) of fresh coriander

juice of ½ lemon

about 3–4 tablespoons olive oil, or as needed

For the tahini yogurt

6 tablespoons Greek-style yogurt (not the thick sort) or plant-based yogurt

4 tablespoons tahini

Preheat the oven to 220°C (200°C fan), Gas Mark 7. Line a large baking tray with baking paper.

Place the sweet potato slices on the lined tray. Drizzle the slices with the olive oil, sprinkle over the ras el hanout and add a generous amount of salt, then use your hands to rub the mixture evenly all over them. Spread out in a single layer and roast for 30 minutes or until cooked through.

Meanwhile, for the herb oil, put the herbs, lemon juice, olive oil (enough to enable the mixture to spin) and some salt and pepper into a blender and blitz until smooth.

Mix the yogurt and tahini together in a small bowl and season well with salt and pepper.

Remove the sweet potatoes from the oven and transfer to a platter. Pour over the tahini yogurt followed by the herb oil. Scatter with the pine nuts and pomegranate seeds and serve.

Serve with Spicy Keema Rolls (see page 73) or Pan-fried Salmon with Barberry Butter (see page 133).

Spice-roasted Potatoes with, Tomato, Pepper & Harissa Sauce

This is a lovely dish that makes the potato feel less of a side-show act and more of a star. Think of it as comfort food with a Middle Eastern twist, which can very well stand alone but, for the creative among you, can easily be paired with fried eggs, halloumi or even simply some crumbled feta on top.

SERVES 6

1kg potatoes, peeled and cut into
    2.5cm cubes

2 teaspoons paprika

2 teaspoons ground turmeric

2 teaspoons cumin seeds

3 tablespoons garlic oil or olive oil

Maldon sea salt flakes and freshly
    ground black pepper

handful of chopped mint, parsley,
    fresh coriander or dill, to garnish

crumbled feta, to serve (optional)

For the sauce

olive oil

2 garlic cloves, bashed and thinly
    sliced

250g (drained weight) roasted
    red peppers from a jar, roughly
    chopped

400g can chopped tomatoes

1 heaped tablespoon rose harissa

1 tablespoon caster sugar

Preheat the oven to 220°C (200°C fan), Gas Mark 7. Line a baking tray with baking paper. Place the potato pieces on the lined tray. Mix the spices and garlic oil or olive oil together and drizzle over the pieces, then use your hands to coat them evenly in the spiced oil. Spread out in a single layer, season well with salt and pepper and roast for 30 minutes or until tender and cooked through.

Meanwhile, to make the sauce, drizzle some olive oil into a saucepan, add the garlic slices and cook over a medium heat for 2 minutes. Add the red peppers, tomatoes and rose harissa with a generous amount of salt and cook, stirring, for a further 2 minutes. Add the sugar, stir well and cook over a medium-high heat for 20 minutes, stirring regularly to ensure it doesn't burn. Remove from the heat and using a stick blender, blitz the sauce until smooth. Taste and adjust the seasoning if desired.

Arrange the potatoes on a serving plate, pour the sauce over, then scatter with the herbs and feta (if using).

Serve with Herb Koftas with Warm Yogurt Sauce & Spiced Mint Butter (see page 92) or Butterflied Lamb with Tahini Garlic Yogurt (see page 123).

Potato, Spinach & Egg Fry with Yogurt & Spiced Butter

This is a recipe suitable for breakfast, lunch or dinner. The fried potatoes can carry a multitude of flavours and spices, and this combination is wonderfully simple yet indulgent courtesy of the spice butter finish.

SERVES 2–4

olive oil

500g potatoes, peeled and cut into 1cm cubes

2 teaspoons dried fenugreek leaves

125g baby spinach leaves

5 spring onions, thinly sliced

4 eggs

100g Greek-style yogurt

Maldon sea salt flakes and freshly ground black pepper

For the spiced butter

½ teaspoon coriander seeds

½ teaspoon cumin seeds

1 teaspoon pul biber chilli flakes

30g butter

flatbreads, to serve

For the spiced butter, heat a small dry saucepan over a medium-high heat, add the coriander and cumin seeds and toast for 1–2 minutes until they release their aroma, shaking the pan intermittently to prevent them from burning. Remove from the heat and lightly crush using a pestle and mortar until coarsely ground (not ground down to a powder), tip back into the pan with the pul biber and set aside.

Place a frying pan over a medium-high heat, pour in some olive oil and fry the potatoes until they begin to brown all over, stirring occasionally. Cover the pan with a lid and cook for a further 10 minutes, shaking the pan regularly to prevent the potatoes sticking, until tender. Remove the lid, add the fenugreek and mix to coat the potatoes. Push the potatoes to one side of the pan, add the spinach and cook for 2–3 minutes until wilted, then mix into the potatoes. Add the spring onions and season everything well with salt and pepper. Make 4 wells in the potato mixture and crack an egg into each one, then reduce to a gentle medium heat, replace the lid and cook for 5–6 minutes.

Melt the butter in the pan with the spices and season with salt and pepper. Once the eggs are cooked, dollop with the yogurt, then pour the spiced butter over and serve with flatbreads and a grinding of black pepper. This needs no accompaniment.

Spiced Tahini & Honey-roasted Aubergines

Since adopting this technique, I have glazed aubergines with every conceivable kind of sauce you could imagine. This method is so incredibly good for cooking aubergines that it should give you the confidence to experiment with other flavours, and I would encourage you to do just that. But while you're here, this is a fantastic combination of ingredients that gives a rich, nutty and chewy surface when slightly cooled. I ask you, what's not to love about that?

MAKES 4

2 large aubergines

4 tablespoons garlic oil

3 tablespoons tahini

2 tablespoons clear honey (if vegan, use maple syrup)

1 teaspoon garlic granules

1 teaspoon pul biber chilli flakes

Maldon sea salt flakes and freshly ground black pepper

Preheat the oven to 200°C (180°C fan), Gas Mark 6. Line a baking tray with baking paper.

Using a sharp knife, cut the aubergines in half lengthways, then score a criss-cross pattern in the cut sides and place, cut-side up, on the lined tray. Brush the scored flesh of each half with the garlic oil and roast for 30 minutes or until cooked through.

Meanwhile, mix together the tahini, honey (or maple syrup), garlic granules, pul biber and a generous amount of salt and pepper in a small bowl until smooth.

Remove the aubergines from the oven, divide the tahini mixture between the halves and spread all over each surface. Roast for a further 10–12 minutes until lovely and golden brown on the surface. Remove from the oven and serve.

Serve with Halloumi, Blood Orange & Pistachio Rocket Salad (see page 18) or Nargessi Kofta Loaf (see page 107).

Roasted Aubergines with Spicy Peanut Sauce

When I consider the aubergine, I often wonder how many more aubergine recipes I have left in me. Then I think of another flavour combination (usually inspired by what's in my store cupboard) that I think may work well, and the rest, as they say, is history. Aubergines are endlessly versatile, and this dish inspired by satay sauce flavours – plus the heat of harissa – works so well. Please trust me and make it for yourself!

SERVES 4

2 large aubergines, quartered
 lengthways
olive oil

For the sauce

2 tablespoons smooth peanut butter
2 tablespoons clear honey (if vegan,
 use maple syrup)
1 tablespoon rose harissa
1 tablespoon rice vinegar
1 tablespoon lukewarm water
Maldon sea salt flakes

To serve

generous handful of salted peanuts,
 roughly chopped
2 spring onions, thinly sliced from root
 to tip
good handful of chopped fresh
 coriander leaves

Preheat the oven to 200°C (180°C fan), Gas Mark 6. Line a baking tray with baking paper.

Place the aubergines on the lined tray, rub the exposed flesh with olive oil and roast for 30 minutes until soft and cooked through.

Meanwhile, for the sauce, put the peanut butter, honey (or maple syrup), harissa, vinegar and a good pinch of salt into a small bowl and mix together. Then add the water to thin the mixture down and mix well.

Once cooked, arrange the roasted aubergines on a platter. Drizzle with the sauce, scatter with the peanuts, spring onions and coriander and serve.

Serve with Spicy Keema Rolls (see page 73) or Sweet Potato & Chickpea Balls (see page 86).

Traybaked Spicy Chickpeas & Aubergines with Yogurt & Herbs

The convenience of cooking everything together in the oven on one tray appeals to me greatly and means I can disappear for a while and get on with other things. This dish can even be served straight from the oven to the table. Why bother with the extra washing-up when it will only get devoured in minutes anyway!

SERVES 4–6

1 teaspoon paprika

1 teaspoon ground turmeric

1 teaspoon ground cumin

1 teaspoon ground coriander

olive oil

400g can chickpeas, drained

2 large aubergines, peeled, halved widthways and cut into 2.5cm-thick wedges

Maldon sea salt flakes and freshly ground black pepper

To serve

150g Greek-style yogurt or plant-based yogurt

generous handful of chopped mixed herb leaves (I used a mix of fresh coriander, dill and mint leaves)

3 tablespoons tahini, thinned down with lukewarm water

3 tablespoons pomegranate molasses

generous handful of shop-bought crispy fried onions

Preheat the oven to 200°C (180°C fan), Gas Mark 6. Line your largest baking tray with baking paper.

Put all the spices, 3 tablespoons olive oil and a generous amount of salt and pepper into a mixing bowl and mix together. Add the chickpeas and mix until evenly combined.

Spread the aubergine wedges out on the lined tray in a single layer, drizzle generously with olive oil and rub in all over, then season well with salt and pepper. Make some space to add the chickpeas to the tray in a single layer – try to avoid covering the aubergines. Roast for 30–35 minutes until nicely browned all over. Remove from the oven, and transfer to a platter if you prefer.

Ensure the yogurt is a pouring consistency, adding a little lukewarm water to thin it down if necessary, then pour all over the roasted aubergines and chickpeas. Scatter over the herbs and drizzle over the loosened tahini, top with the pomegranate molasses and then the crispy onions and serve.

Serve with Spicy Keema Rolls (see page 73) or Dried Lime & Spice Marinated Lamb Chops (see page 95).

Roasted Tomatoes with Labneh & Sumac Spice Oil

One of the most classic Persian accompaniments is the whole flame-roasted tomato. A staple served with every kebab, it's simply made by placing a whole tomato on a charcoal grill and roasting until the skin is somewhat charred in parts and the soft flesh inside is bursting with juices. This dish is inspired by my love for the roasted tomato, but reimagined for indoor cooking. Served with labneh (which Persians serve with everything) and a little spice oil for adding depth and flavour, it really is a wonderful dish and perfect alongside roasted or barbecued meats and vegetables.

SERVES 4–6

2 very large and 4–6 medium
    tomatoes, halved
olive oil
500g labneh or thick Greek yogurt
    or plant-based yogurt
Maldon sea salt flakes and freshly
    ground black pepper

For the spice oil
4–5 tablespoons olive oil
3 garlic cloves, thinly sliced
1 teaspoon fennel seeds
1 teaspoon cumin seeds
1 teaspoon sumac
1 teaspoon pul biber chilli flakes

Preheat your oven to its highest setting. Line a large baking tray with baking paper.

Place the tomato halves, cut-side up, on the lined tray and drizzle with olive oil. Roast for 20–25 minutes or until nicely charred, then remove from the oven and set aside.

For the spice oil, place a small saucepan over a gentle medium heat, add the olive oil, garlic slices and fennel and cumin seeds and cook gently for 8–10 minutes until the garlic is cooked but not browned too much. Remove from the heat, add the sumac and pul biber, season with salt and pepper and stir to combine.

Spread the labneh or yogurt out on a large platter until it reaches the edges, then arrange the roasted tomatoes over the labneh or yogurt and season with salt and pepper. Pour the spice oil over and serve.

Serve with Afghani Polow (see page 191) or Dampokhtak (see page 196).

Turmeric-spiced Yogurt with White Beans

This is one of those recipes that shouldn't work – but it does. Spiced beans, fried in a pan, enrobed in yogurt and cooked until the yogurt is hot. If the yogurt curdles slightly then this is nothing to worry about and will still taste just as nice. Really easy, really delicious and unlike anything I've tasted before, it's perfect on toast or with flatbreads.

SERVES 4–6

2 tablespoons olive oil

2 teaspoons cumin seeds

2 teaspoons coriander seeds

2 x 400g cans cannellini beans, drained and rinsed

2 garlic cloves, minced

2 teaspoons ground turmeric

½ teaspoon chilli flakes

200g Greek yogurt or plant-based yogurt

Maldon sea salt flakes and freshly ground black pepper

Heat a large frying pan over a medium-high heat, add the olive oil then the cumin and coriander seeds and fry for a couple of minutes.

Add the beans and garlic and mix to coat them in the spice oil. Add the turmeric, chilli flakes and a generous amount of salt and pepper, mix again and cook for a few minutes.

Stir in the yogurt and keep gently stirring it through the beans while you cook for a few more minutes until the yogurt sauce has reduced and just about coats the beans, then serve seasoned with extra black pepper.

Serve with Nargessi Kofta Loaf (see page 107) or Marinated Halloumi Skewers (see page 162).

Tomato & Feta Fritters

This has a very Greek vibe to it. I love tomatoes and feta together, so combining them in these fritters was a no-brainer. The punch of tarragon is also really lovely with the tomato combo, and I hope you like these as much as I do. I love to serve them with a sort of tzatziki sauce without the cucumber, as below.

MAKES 10–12

500g large plum tomatoes, deseeded

1 teaspoon dried wild oregano

10g tarragon, leaves finely chopped

100g feta cheese, crumbled

5 spring onions, thinly sliced

6 tablespoons plain flour

1 teaspoon baking powder

vegetable oil, for frying

Maldon sea salt flakes and freshly
    ground black pepper

For the sauce

150g Greek-style yogurt

1 small garlic clove, crushed

1 teaspoon dried wild oregano

Pat dry the tomato flesh with kitchen paper, then roughly chop into small cubes and put into a mixing bowl, leaving any remaining liquid behind. Add the oregano, tarragon and some salt and pepper and mix together really well. Leave to sit for 5 minutes, then stir again before adding the feta and spring onions and mixing to combine. Add the flour and baking powder and mix together with a spoon until you have a batter, then set aside.

Meanwhile, mix the sauce ingredients together in a small bowl and season with salt and pepper.

Heat a large frying pan over a medium-high heat, pour in about 2.5cm vegetable oil and bring to frying temperature (add a little bit of the batter: if it sizzles immediately, the oil is hot enough). Line a large plate with a double layer of kitchen paper.

Mix the batter again with the spoon and test to see if you can scoop up a tablespoonful and lightly pat it into a ball – you may need a little more flour to bind the mixture, so add sparingly. Form the batter into 10–12 balls, add to the hot oil and fry in batches gently for a couple of minutes or so on each side until crisp and browned. Remove with a slotted spoon and transfer to the paper-lined plate to drain. Serve with the sauce alongside.

Serve with Herb Koftas with Warm Yogurt Sauce & Spiced Mint Butter (see page 92) or Mama Ghanoush (see page 158).

Sweet & Spicy Crunchy Aubergines

When I first made this recipe, I wanted to shout it from the rooftops because it was so insanely delicious that I felt it needed to be shared. The wonderful flavour of the Thai holy basil really takes it to the next level, and the crunchy coating gives the aubergine an extra dimension. I can eat a whole pan of this with just some steamed rice on the side: no other accompaniment is needed to keep me happy.

SERVES 4

vegetable oil, for frying

2 large aubergines, peeled, halved widthways and cut into 2cm-thick batons

7 tablespoons cornflour

6 fat garlic cloves, thinly sliced

2 heaped tablespoons rose harissa

3 tablespoons caster sugar

juice of 1 fat lime

3 tablespoons light soy sauce

250ml cold water

leaves from 1 small packet (about 30g) of fresh Thai holy basil (or use ordinary basil or fresh coriander)

Maldon sea salt flakes and freshly ground black pepper

Heat a large, deep frying pan over a medium-high heat, pour in 2.5cm vegetable oil and bring to frying temperature (add a breadcrumb: if it sizzles, the oil is hot enough). Line a plate with a double layer of kitchen paper.

Put the aubergines, 6 tablespoons of the cornflour and a very generous seasoning of salt and pepper into a mixing bowl and stir together, ensuring the cornflour coats the aubergines all over, leaving no cornflour behind.

Add the aubergine batons to the hot oil and fry a few at a time in 2–3 batches for a good few minutes until they are nicely browned on all sides. You don't want to brown the outside too quickly as the aubergine flesh inside won't be cooked, so if necessary, allow the oil to cool down a little before frying the next batch. Remove the cooked batches with a slotted spoon and transfer to the paper-lined plate to drain.

Heat a saucepan over a medium heat, drizzle in 2 tablespoons of oil and fry the garlic slices until translucent and lightly sizzling. Add the harissa, sugar, lime juice, soy sauce and remaining tablespoon of cornflour and mix together well. Gradually pour in the water, mixing well until evenly combined, and cook until the sauce looks glossy and has reduced in consistency. Stir in the Thai basil leaves, then add the crunchy aubergines, working carefully and quickly to coat them in the sauce. Serve immediately.

Serve with Charred Broccoli with Lemons, Chillies & Yogurt (see page 154) or Marinated Halloumi Skewers (see page 162).

Tangy Pomegranate & Tomato Aubergines

This recipe feels familiar in a chutney sort of way – almost like a fresh aubergine chutney that's more of a side dish than merely a relish or sauce. Some earthy spicing and sweetness rounded off with the sharp tang of pomegranate molasses make this a perfect dish to cut through the richness of roasted meats and kebabs. It's also great with toasted pitta or sourdough.

SERVES 4

olive oil

1 large onion, finely chopped

4 fat garlic cloves, thinly sliced

1 teaspoon fennel seeds

1 teaspoon cumin seeds

1 teaspoon ground turmeric

3 large aubergines, smoked (see page 142 for method), peeled and flesh drained of excess liquid

2 tablespoons tomato purée

5 tablespoons pomegranate molasses

2 tablespoons vegan red wine vinegar

2 tablespoons caster sugar

Maldon sea salt flakes and freshly ground black pepper

toasted pitta, to serve

Heat a frying pan over a medium heat, add a good drizzle of olive oil and cook the onion and garlic until softened. Stir in the fennel and cumin seeds followed by the turmeric and mix well. Add the cooked aubergine flesh and a generous amount of salt and pepper and mix really well. Then add the tomato purée, pomegranate molasses, vinegar and sugar and again mix really well until all is evenly combined. Cook, stirring regularly, for 10–15 minutes.

Reduce the heat slightly and leave to cook for a further 20 minutes or so, stirring occasionally. Taste and adjust the seasoning if desired. Serve warm with toasted pitta.

Serve with Afghani Polow (see page 191) or Minced Lamb Börek (see page 103).

Pasta,
Noodles
& Grains

Baghala Polow with Saffron Lamb Shanks

This recipe holds so many memories for me, as my grandmother's sister, Khaleh (Aunty) Gohar Malek, was the only really good cook in our family, and whenever she made this it was pure joy in every mouthful. The smell, the glistening buttery rice, those juicy, soft lamb shanks flecked with saffron . . . it instantly transports me back to my childhood. For many years I was scared to recreate it, and it took me a long time to perfect the recipe. If you are vegetarian you can leave out the meat, but for me, pouring the juices from the lamb over the rice and *tahdig* (crispy base) is literally one of my greatest pleasures.

SERVES 6

olive oil

6 fat garlic cloves, thinly sliced

400g peeled fresh broad beans

7 tablespoons dried dill

75g butter

500g basmati rice

2–3 tablespoons ghee (or vegetable oil if you prefer)

0.5g (½ teaspoon) best-quality saffron threads, plus an extra pinch

Maldon sea salt flakes and freshly ground black pepper

For the lamb shanks

vegetable oil

2 onions, halved and thinly sliced into half moons

0.5g (½ teaspoon) Iranian saffron threads, ground to a powder using a pestle and mortar

6 fat garlic cloves, bashed and peeled

4 large lamb shanks

For the lamb shanks, place a large saucepan over a medium heat, add some vegetable oil and fry the onions until beginning to soften but not brown. Add the saffron and cook for a few minutes, stirring regularly. Then add the garlic cloves and the lamb shanks along with a generous amount of salt and pepper and turn the shanks to coat them in the onion mixture, taking care not to let anything brown. Cook for 10–15 minutes, turning the shanks over halfway through. Pour over enough boiling water to cover the shanks, then reduce to a medium heat and cook, covered with a lid, for 2½ hours until tender and the meat is falling away from the bone. Check and turn over the shanks occasionally to ensure the meat is submerged, and add more water if necessary.

Meanwhile, heat a large frying pan over a medium heat, drizzle in some olive oil and fry the garlic slices until soft. Add the broad beans and dried dill, season heavily with salt and pepper (because you will be seasoning 500g rice) and then add the butter. Stir and then cook the beans for 10–15 minutes. Remove from the heat and set aside.

continued overleaf

Bring a separate large saucepan of water to the boil. Add the rice and stir to avoid the grains from sticking together, then parboil for about 6–7 minutes until the grains turn from a dullish off-white colour to a more opaque, brilliant white and have slightly elongated. Drain and immediately rinse thoroughly under cold running water, running your fingers through the rice, until all the grains are well rinsed of starch and completely cooled. Drain the rice thoroughly by shaking the sieve well, then leave for any remaining water to drain for 10 minutes. Shake off any excess water before use.

Scrunch up a large square of baking paper, then smooth out and line the base of the rice pan (but no need to line if the pan is nonstick). Place the pan over a gentle heat, add the ghee (or vegetable oil) and allow the ghee to melt. If using a gas hob, pour in 1cm cold water, and swirl the pan around to mix the ghee (or oil) and water together to prevent the rice from burning (you can omit this if using an electric/induction hob). Season with salt, then loosely scatter just enough rice into the pan to coat the base in an even layer. Mix the rest of the rice with the broad bean mixture, crumble in the saffron and fold through, then scatter (do not press) into the pan and spread out to the sides. Using the handle of a wooden spoon, poke lots of holes in the rice, piercing all the way to the bottom of the pan. Wrap the pan lid in a clean tea towel so that it fits snugly on the pan. If using a gas hob, cook over the lowest flame for 45 minutes. If using an electric/induction hob, cook over a medium heat for 1–1¼ hours.

Once the rice and lamb are cooked, take the remaining pinch of saffron and using a pestle and mortar, grind it in a small bowl. Stir in a teaspoon of boiling water, then add a generous handful of the cooked rice and mix until the grains are all bright yellow.

Spoon the cooked rice out on to a serving platter and scatter over the handful of saffron-tinted rice. Remove the crispy *tahdig* crust from the bottom of the pan, break it up and serve it around the rice. To serve, you can either break off some of the meat and serve the pieces of lamb folded into the rice with some of the juice from the shanks poured over, or serve the lamb and juices on the side. I also like to serve this as a soup using the remaining meat juices and some of the rice.

Serve with Burnt Courgettes with Lemon & Feta Yogurt (see page 145).

Afghani Polow

This is a recipe from my childhood that my Afghani Uncle Nehad's mum would make for us when we came round for lunch. My mum and I always just called it Afghani *polow* (rice), and years later I looked everywhere for a recipe or recreation of the dish in Afghani restaurants only to be told that the one they have is with carrots (and sometimes raisins) and lamb, and is called *ghabboli polow* (a similar recipe for which is in my book *Sirocco*). I have thankfully managed to prise the spice mix that was used to make the rice out of my Aunty Azita, but was otherwise very much left to my own devices to experiment and perfect the recipe. While nothing could ever be as great as the real thing, it's a darned good second, and much like I did when I was a child, my own family loves it!

SERVES 4–6

vegetable oil

2 onions, finely chopped

800g boneless lamb shoulder, cut into 1cm cubes

1 heaped teaspoon ground cinnamon

1 teaspoon ground cumin

1 teaspoon ground coriander

½ teaspoon cayenne pepper

¼ teaspoon ground cloves

¼ teaspoon ground nutmeg

6 fat garlic cloves, thinly sliced

75g butter

600g basmati rice

2–3 tablespoons ghee (or vegetable oil)

Maldon sea salt flakes and freshly ground black pepper

Place a saucepan over a medium-high heat, pour in a generous amount of vegetable oil and fry the onions until translucent and beginning to brown around the edges. Add the lamb, spices and garlic and stir well to coat the meat in the spices, then season heavily with salt and pepper. Cover the pan with a lid but leave a gap open, reduce to a gentle medium heat and cook for an hour, stirring occasionally to prevent sticking. Remove the lid, add the butter and increase the heat to reduce any excess liquid so that there is just enough to coat the meat (this should happen pretty quickly because there shouldn't be much liquid anyway), but keep an eye on it and stir occasionally to prevent burning. Remove from the heat and set aside.

Bring a large saucepan of water to the boil. Add the rice and stir to avoid the grains from sticking together, then parboil for about 6–7 minutes until the grains turn from a dullish off-white colour to a more opaque, brilliant white and have slightly elongated. Drain and immediately rinse thoroughly under cold running water, running your fingers through the rice, until all the grains are well rinsed of starch and completely cooled. Drain the rice thoroughly by shaking the sieve well, then leave for any remaining water to drain for 10 minutes. Shake off any excess water before use. Rinse the rice saucepan.

continued overleaf

Scrunch up a large square of baking paper, then smooth out and line the base of the rice pan (you can omit this if your pan is nonstick). Place the pan over a gentle heat, add the ghee (or vegetable oil) and allow the ghee to melt. If using a gas hob, pour in 1cm cold water, and swirl the pan around to mix the ghee (or oil) and water together to prevent the rice from burning (you can omit this if using an electric/induction hob). Season with salt, then loosely scatter just enough rice into the pan to coat the base in an even layer. Mix the rest of the rice with the meat mixture, then scatter (do not press) into the pan and spread out to the sides. Using the handle of a wooden spoon, poke lots of holes in the rice, piercing all the way to the base of the pan. Wrap the pan lid in a clean tea towel so that it fits snugly on the pan. If using a gas hob, cook over the lowest flame for 1–1¼ hours. If using an electric/induction hob, cook over a medium heat for 2–2½ hours.

Once cooked, remove the lid and spread the rice out to create a flat base. Spoon out the polow into a serving bowl or on a platter. If there is any crispy *tahdig* crust, then serve it on top of the rice.

Serve with Burnt Courgettes with Lemon & Feta Yogurt (see page 145) or Roasted Tomatoes with Labneh & Sumac Spice Oil (see page 177).

Cheat's Zereshk Polow

Zereshk is the Persian word for barberries, those tiny sour red berries that I love and which feature in various recipes of mine, and this is the classic recipe that they are used for, albeit a simplified, cheat's version for you to enjoy. This is the version I make the most at home because when the craving hits, I need the speediest solution to curb my appetite. Traditionally the rice would be cooked in the Persian way and served with slow-braised chicken cooked with saffron and onions, but a whole roast chicken or poussin is a great choice, too.

SERVES 4

0.5g (½ teaspoon) best-quality saffron threads

1 tablespoon boiling water

250g basmati rice

25g butter

50g dried barberries

4 tablespoons (approximately 60g) caster sugar

Maldon sea salt flakes

Using a pestle and mortar, grind the saffron down with some sea salt flakes for abrasion, then transfer to a cup. Pour over the boiling water, stir and leave to sit until required.

Cook the basmati rice in a large saucepan of boiling water according to the packet instructions, making sure not to overcook it. Drain and immediately rinse thoroughly under cold running water, running your fingers through the rice, until all the grains are well rinsed of starch and completely cooled. Drain the rice thoroughly by shaking the sieve well, then leave for 10 minutes to allow any remaining water to drain. Shake off any excess water before use.

Melt the butter in a small saucepan over a gentle heat, add the barberries and stir them for a minute or two until they begin to plump up. Once they have turned a brighter shade of red, add the sugar and stir until dissolved, then remove immediately from the heat.

Place a generous handful of the cooked rice in a small bowl, pour over the saffron solution and mix until the grains are all bright yellow. Return the rest of the cooked rice to its saucepan over a medium heat, then add the barberry and butter mixture and a generous seasoning of salt and mix well. Stir in the saffron-tinted rice, and once everything is hot, pile on to a platter and serve.

Serve with Chicken, Apricot, Orange & Almond Tagine (see page 91) or Ras el Hanout Sticky Spatchcock Poussin (see page 118).

Dampokhtak

This is a dish that reminds me of my grandmother, as it was one of the few things she would cook, so I felt compelled to nail this recipe and honour her memory –Ezat Malek, I hope I have done you proud.

SERVES 6–8

200g dried split broad beans

500g basmati rice

olive oil

2 large onions, finely chopped

8 garlic cloves, very thinly sliced

50g salted butter

2 tablespoons ground turmeric

250ml cold water

2 tablespoons ghee

3 tablespoons Greek-style yogurt

Maldon sea salt flakes and freshly
ground black pepper

Soak the dried beans in cold water for 3 hours, then rinse very well, drain and set aside.

Bring a large saucepan of water to the boil. Add the rice and stir to avoid the grains from sticking together, then parboil for about 6–7 minutes until the grains turn from a dullish off-white colour to a more opaque, brilliant white and have slightly elongated. Drain and immediately rinse thoroughly under cold running water, running your fingers through the rice, until all the grains are well rinsed of starch and completely cooled. Drain the rice thoroughly by shaking the sieve well, then leave for 10 minutes to allow any remaining water to drain. Shake off any excess water before use.

Place a large frying pan over a medium heat, drizzle in enough olive oil to cover the base of the pan and fry the onions until softened. Add the garlic slivers and fry for a couple more minutes. Then add the soaked beans, butter, turmeric and some pepper and mix well to coat the beans. Pour in the cold water and mix again, then leave to cook for about 15 minutes, stirring regularly to make sure the beans don't stick. Remove from the heat – don't worry, the beans won't be fully cooked at this stage.

Place the rice pan over a low flame if using a gas hob or gentle medium heat if using an electric/induction hob. Add the ghee, and once melted, add the yogurt, some salt and 3 handfuls of the drained rice and mix well. Shake the pan to coat the rice in the yogurt, then pat down to coat the base of the pan. Mix the rest of the rice with the bean mixture, scatter (do not press) into the pan and spread out to the sides. Using the handle of a wooden spoon, poke lots of holes in the rice, piercing all the way to the base of the pan. Wrap the pan lid in a clean tea towel so that it fits snugly on the pan. If using a gas hob, cook the rice for 45 minutes. If using an electric/induction hob, cook for 1½ hours. Either flip or spoon out the rice to serve.

Serve with Roasted Tomatoes with Labneh & Sumac Spice Oil (see page 177).

Creamy Spiced Sausage Pasta,

This is a lovely pasta dish, gently spiced but with so much flavour that it makes it impossible to put down. I love using sausagemeat in pastas, as it reminds me of all the wonderful Italian pastas and pizzas I've enjoyed over the years. As the sauce is beautifully rich, a little goes a long way – but then again, I can be terribly greedy and make this batch just for two.

SERVES 3–4

400g good-quality sausages with a high meat content (flavour of your choice)

1 teaspoon fennel seeds

1 teaspoon cumin seeds

olive oil

4 fat garlic cloves, thinly sliced

2 teaspoons dried wild oregano

2 teaspoons pul biber chilli flakes

400g can chopped tomatoes

1 teaspoon caster sugar

125g mascarpone cheese

300g pasta shape of your choice (I like spirals and rigatoni tubes)

Maldon sea salt flakes and freshly ground black pepper,

grated Parmesan cheese, to serve (optional)

Using a sharp knife, score the sausages and remove the outer casing, then pinch off the sausagemeat into about 6 pieces per sausage.

Heat a large dry saucepan over a medium-high heat, add the fennel and cumin seeds and toast for a couple of minutes until they release their aroma, shaking the pan intermittently to prevent them from burning. Then add a generous drizzle of olive oil and fry the garlic slices until translucent but not coloured. Add the sausage pieces and fry for 4–5 minutes until sealed and coloured all over the outside, shaking the pan to move and turn them. Next, add the oregano, pul biber and a generous amount of salt and pepper before adding the tomatoes and sugar and stirring well. Fill the empty tomato can halfway with water, swish it around and pour into the sauce, then reduce the heat to a medium simmer and cook for 30 minutes, stirring occasionally. Finally, stir the mascarpone into the sauce until evenly incorporated.

Towards the end of the sauce cooking time, cook the pasta in a large saucepan of salted boiling water according to the packet instructions, then drain, reserving some of the cooking water.

Add the pasta to the sauce and toss to coat. Cook for a couple of minutes, then check and taste and adjust the seasoning if desired, adding a little of the reserved pasta water if you need a bit more liquid. Serve immediately and shower with grated Parmesan, if desired. This needs no accompaniment.

Harissa, Tahini & Lamb Spaghetti

By now you will know that I never feel compelled to limit my pasta use to Italian recipes. This is the kind of recipe that comes together pretty easily and is a deeply comforting, spiced bowl of spaghetti with all the familiarity of a good meat and spag combo but with wildly different flavours. I don't like using the word 'fusion' because it infers intent to purposely blend one thing into another . . . all I know is this kind of food tastes great to me and has notes that hit every spot on my satisfaction scale. If you feel like making your noodles a little more soupy, simply add more of the pasta cooking water or a light vegetable stock to increase the final volume of liquid.

SERVES 4

vegetable oil

1 large onion, finely chopped

6 fat garlic cloves, finely sliced

500g minced lamb

1 tablespoon garlic granules

1 tablespoon curry powder

1 tablespoon ground cumin

2 tablespoons rose harissa

3 tablespoons tahini

3 tablespoons light soy sauce

300g spaghetti

4 spring onions, finely sliced diagonally
   from root to tip

2 tablespoons toasted sesame seeds

Maldon sea salt flakes and freshly
   ground black pepper

Place a large frying pan over a medium-high heat, add a drizzle of vegetable oil and fry the onion until soft and translucent, then stir in the garlic slices and cook for 2 minutes to soften. Add the minced lamb and immediately break it up as finely as possible to prevent it cooking in clumps, then stir in the garlic granules and dry spices until incorporated into the mince. Continue cooking the mince, stirring as you go. Add the harissa, tahini, soy sauce and salt and pepper and mix everything together until evenly combined.

Cook the spaghetti in a large saucepan of salted boiling water according to the packet instructions, then drain, reserving some of the cooking water.

Add the spaghetti to the lamb mixture and mix well, then pour in enough of the reserved pasta water to make the mixture a little soupy. Finally, add the spring onions and sesame seeds, mix together and serve scattered with the chopped coriander. This needs no accompaniment.

Punchy Pepper, Tomato & Pasta Soup

When I think of soups, I think of my mother. I'd like to tell you a fondly recalled tale about how she always made soups for me when I was growing up and they were the best I'd ever tasted, but the truth is, beyond opening a can and reheating its contents, my mother has never made a soup from scratch in her life; however, she loves soup more than most people do. This recipe relies heavily on store-cupboard ingredients for its flavour, it's lovely and punchy, and the orzo pasta makes it more of a meal than just a soup.

SERVES 4

olive oil

1 large onion, finely chopped

4 tablespoons tomato purée

4 fat garlic cloves, thinly sliced

1 green pepper, cored, deseeded and halved, then cut widthways into thin strips

1 tablespoon dried wild oregano

1 tablespoon dried mint

1 teaspoon pul biber chilli flakes

75g orzo pasta

30g butter (optional)

1.2 litres boiling water

4 spring onions, thinly sliced from root to tip

Maldon sea salt flakes and freshly ground black pepper

Place a medium saucepan over a medium-high heat, drizzle in enough olive oil to just coat the base and fry the onion until translucent and beginning to colour around the edges.

Mix the tomato purée into the onion and cook for a few minutes, stirring regularly to ensure it doesn't stick. Add the garlic, green pepper, herbs, pul biber and a generous amount of salt and pepper and cook, stirring well, for a couple of minutes.

Add the orzo and butter (or a drizzle of olive oil for a vegan option) and stir well to coat the orzo and ensure everything is evenly combined, then cook for 4–5 minutes, stirring to prevent sticking. Pour in the boiling water, stir and cook over a medium heat for 25–30 minutes, stirring occasionally, until the orzo is cooked and the soup has reduced nicely.

Stir in the spring onions, then taste and adjust the seasoning if desired. This needs no accompaniment.

Nut Butter Noodles

I first came across peanut noodles thanks to the great Nigella Lawson, whose recipes have provided me with so much satisfaction and inspiration over the years. Nigella knows good food and introduced many of us to the art of being a home cook, making it undaunting and accessible in a way that nobody had quite managed to do before her. This dish switches it up with the addition of coconut milk and garlic, and – of course! – also features nigella seeds. Credit where credit is due, Nigella continues to inspire me, and I make her recipes at home more than anybody else's. This dish is best eaten as soon as it has been made.

SERVES 4–6

200g medium egg noodles

2 tablespoons sesame seeds

6 tablespoons crunchy peanut butter

2 tablespoons soy sauce

2 tablespoons caster sugar

200ml coconut milk

2 garlic cloves, minced

juice of ½ lime

Maldon sea salt flakes and freshly
    ground black pepper

To serve

½ teaspoon nigella seeds

1 teaspoon pul biber chilli flakes

5 spring onions, thinly sliced
    diagonally from root to tip

good handful of fresh coriander leaves

Cook the noodles according to the packet instructions, then drain, rinse in cold water, drain again and set aside.

Heat a dry frying pan over a medium heat, add the sesame seeds and toast for a few minutes until nicely golden brown. Remove from the pan and set aside.

Place a small saucepan over a gentle medium heat, add the peanut butter, soy sauce, sugar, coconut milk, garlic and lime juice mix well. Season with salt and pepper and heat through until hot but not bubbling. If the mixture is too thick, thin it down with some water or milk.

Pour the warm peanut sauce over the noodles and then toss with the toasted sesame seeds. Serve on a flat plate, scattered with the nigella seeds, pul biber, spring onions and coriander, and eat immediately (as delicious as it is, once cold it will set and need warming through to revive it).

Serve with Tamarind Chicken Wings (see page 65) or Cod Flavour Bombs (see page 77).

Spiced Coconut Chicken & Noodle Stew

Coconut is one of my favourite flavours – from fresh coconut and desiccated to juice and coconut milk, I love all forms. I find the addition of coconut improves most things, but I especially like it in soups and curries. Though this is not a curry, this warming and fragrant stew offers many of the same properties. The addition of noodles reminds me of the famous *khao soi* dish of Northern Thailand and makes this more of a meal, though you can omit the noodles and simply serve it with rice or naan bread.

SERVES 4

vegetable oil

2 onions, roughly chopped

600g boneless, skinless chicken thighs

4 green cardamom pods, lightly
   crushed

1 teaspoon cumin seeds

2 teaspoons ground turmeric

2 tablespoons rose harissa

400ml can coconut milk

300g medium egg noodles

Maldon sea salt flakes and freshly
   ground black pepper

To serve (optional)

handful of bean sprouts

lime wedges

chopped fresh coriander leaves

Place a large saucepan over a medium-high heat, drizzle in some vegetable oil and fry the onions until softened and translucent. Add the chicken and dry spices along with a generous amount of salt and pepper and turn to coat the chicken in the onion and spice mixture, then stir-fry for a few minutes. Add the harissa and stir-fry for a few more minutes.

Reduce the heat to a gentle medium simmer, pour in the coconut milk and enough water to just about cover the chicken and stir to combine, then cover the pan with a lid and cook gently for an hour, stirring occasionally to prevent sticking. Keep an eye on the liquid volume, as you want to ensure that the chicken is cooked and tender but also that there is a lovely soupy, creamy broth.

When the stew is ready, cook the noodles according to the packet instructions, then drain and divide between 4 serving bowls.

To serve, pour the stew over the cooked noodles, then add the bean sprouts, lime wedges and coriander if desired. This needs no accompaniment.

Mushroom Spaghetti with Creamy Pistachio & Garlic Sauce

Tahini is invaluable in the kitchen, and brilliant for creating rich, creamy textures in recipes without the need for dairy or meat. Having once had to temporarily cut out both meat and dairy, I was desperate for something that would satisfy me in a way that a comforting creamy pasta would do, and so this recipe was born. Despite being back to my normal eating regimen, I still absolutely love this rich, creamy and delicious recipe.

SERVES 4

500g chestnut mushrooms, quartered

vegetable oil

300g spaghetti

For the sauce

100g pistachio nuts

2 fat garlic cloves, peeled

150ml warm water, or more if needed

2 tablespoons tahini

Maldon sea salt flakes and freshly ground black pepper

Heat a large frying pan or saucepan over a high heat, and once hot, add the mushrooms to the dry pan, allow them to release their liquid and then cook until all the liquid has evaporated. Add a drizzle of oil, then fry until nicely browned in parts, stirring occasionally. Remove the pan from the heat and set aside.

Put all the sauce ingredients into a bullet blender or mini food processor and blitz until as smooth as possible, adding a little more warm water if needed to make the mixture liquid enough to blitz.

Cook the spaghetti in a large saucepan of salted boiling water according to the packet instructions, then drain, reserving some of the cooking water.

Reheat the mushrooms over a medium-high heat and add the sauce, stirring to coat the mushrooms. Taste and adjust the seasoning if desired, then cook the sauce for a couple of minutes. Add the spaghetti and some of the reserved pasta water to the mushroom pan and mix well until the sauce and mushrooms evenly coat the pasta. Add a little more pasta water if needed and some more seasoning to taste, then serve immediately. This needs no accompaniment.

Soup e Jow

My mother adores this Persian soup so much that she begged me to learn how to make it. I did and now it's a house staple that everyone enjoys because even though it is incredibly simple it's really quite comforting, which in my humble opinion is what all the best soups should be. *Jow* is the Persian word for 'barley', and I like to go heavy on the barley because I love the texture once cooked. The final flourish comes from lemon juice, something Persians are obsessed with adding to everything. I will leave this element up to you, but a little lemon does work well with it.

SERVES 3–4

olive oil

1 large onion, very finely diced

1 large carrot, peeled and very finely diced

25g butter

1 tablespoon garlic granules

3 tablespoons plain flour

750ml full-fat or semi-skimmed milk
(but not skimmed)

150g pearl barley

1 litre boiling water

juice of ½ lemon, or to taste

1 tablespoon dried chives (optional)

Maldon sea salt flakes and freshly
ground black pepper

Place a large saucepan over a medium heat, drizzle in some olive oil and fry the onion and carrot until soft but not coloured. Add the butter, garlic granules and a generous amount of salt and pepper, and once the butter has melted, stir in the flour quickly to avoid lumps. Add some of the milk and work the flour paste into it until smooth. Keep adding milk and working in the flour paste until it is evenly combined.

Add the barley, boiling water and any remaining milk, stir really well and cook the soup over a gentle medium heat for 45 minutes or so, stirring occasionally, until the barley is soft and puffed up. Taste and adjust the seasoning if desired and add more liquid if you want to, then stir in the lemon juice to taste. Finally, add the dried chives, if desired, and cook for a few more minutes until they are bright green and soft, then serve. This needs no accompaniment.

Samosa Pasta

I absolutely love lamb samosas. The spicy filling with occasional sweet bursts of peas, the ratio of meat to wonderful crisp pastry – it is literally one of the world's best inventions. But I have often wondered what combining that kind of filling with pasta would taste like, and it's really rather good, I can tell you. We love it in my household, and even though I pack in the spices, the kids love it, too, because, well, they have good taste in food. It's a really simple recipe to make using peas from the freezer and spices and pasta from the cupboards together with some mince . . . perfect midweek supper food.

SERVES 3–4

vegetable oil

1 large onion, finely chopped

250g minced beef

1 heaped teaspoon garlic granules

1 teaspoon cumin seeds

1 teaspoon ground cinnamon

1 teaspoon ground turmeric

1 teaspoon chilli flakes

3 tablespoons tomato purée

200ml warm water

3 handfuls of frozen peas

250g farfalle pasta (or pasta shape of
   your choice)

1 small packet (about 30g) of fresh
   coriander, roughly chopped

Maldon sea salt flakes and freshly
   ground black pepper

Place a large frying pan over a medium-high heat, drizzle in some vegetable oil and fry the onion until nicely browned. Add the minced beef and immediately break it up as finely as you can to prevent it cooking in clumps. Then add the garlic granules, all the spices, the tomato purée and a generous amount of salt and pepper and stir-fry the mince for a few minutes. Pour in the warm water and stir-fry again until mostly evaporated. Lastly, stir in the peas and then turn the heat off.

Cook the pasta in a large saucepan of salted boiling water according to the packet instructions, then drain, reserving a cup of the cooking water. Add the pasta to the spicy beef mixture and place over a medium-high heat. Pour in the reserved pasta water and mix together well. Taste and adjust the seasoning if desired, then add the coriander, stir through and serve. This needs no accompaniment.

Spiced Aubergine & Tomato Pasta

Years ago, I learned of a Southern Italian recipe called *melanzane a funghetto* – aubergines fried in strips, then cooked in a simple tomato sauce with a little garlic. Although utterly delicious in its simplicity, over time my version has evolved with the addition of whole spices and a gentle burst of chilli heat, which sits a little more comfortably in my Middle Eastern repertoire and makes for a fantastic pasta dish.

SERVES 4–5

3 large aubergines, peeled and cut into 1.5 x 5–6cm batons

olive oil

1 teaspoon cumin seeds

1 teaspoon fennel seeds

1 head of garlic, cloves separated and thinly sliced

300g baby plum or small tomatoes, halved

2 teaspoons pul biber chilli flakes

1 heaped teaspoon garlic granules

400g can chopped tomatoes

2 teaspoons caster sugar

400g spaghetti

Maldon sea salt flakes and freshly ground black pepper

Parmesan-style vegetarian or vegan cheese to serve (optional)

Preheat the oven to 200°C (180°C fan), Gas Mark 6. Line your largest baking tray with baking paper.

Spread the aubergines out on the lined tray in a single layer, drizzle generously with olive oil and roast for 35–40 minutes until nicely browned all over but not dried out.

Meanwhile, heat a large dry frying pan or saucepan over a medium heat, add the cumin and fennel seeds and toast for a couple of minutes, then drizzle in enough olive oil to coat the base. Add the garlic slices and fry for a couple of minutes until softened and translucent. Add the fresh tomatoes, pul biber, garlic granules and a generous amount of salt and pepper and mix really well, then cook for a few minutes. Add the canned tomatoes and sugar and stir well. Fill the empty tomato can with water, pour into the sauce and stir again, then cook on a rolling simmer for about 30 minutes until nicely thickened.

Once the aubergines are done, remove from the oven. Taste the sauce and adjust the seasoning if desired, then stir in the roasted aubergines.

Cook the spaghetti in a large saucepan of salted boiling water according to the packet instructions, then drain, reserving some of the cooking water. Add the spaghetti to the sauce and toss to coat, adding a little of the reserved pasta water if needed to emulsify the mixture. Serve immediately, with grated vegetarian cheese on top if desired. This needs no accompaniment.

Sweet

Apple Fritters with Cinnamon Sugar

I must confess, I am not the biggest fan of frying things unless it is absolutely worth the end result. These apple fritters are most definitely worth it. How can a handful of ingredients create such joy? Trust me, they do . . . Needless to say, you can substitute the apples with bananas or mix and match, but I really do like the texture and burst of sweetness that comes from using apples, and cinnamon seems to be the perfect partner for them, too.

SERVES 4

100g plain flour

2 teaspoons baking powder

110ml cold water

vegetable oil, or frying

2 apples (I use Braeburn)

For the cinnamon sugar

6 tablespoons caster sugar

2 teaspoons ground cinnamon

Mix the sugar and cinnamon together in a small bowl.

Mix the flour and baking powder together in a mixing bowl. Using a hand whisk, gradually beat in the cold water gently until you have a smooth batter but without overbeating (otherwise the batter will be heavy).

Heat a large, deep frying pan over a medium-high heat, pour in about 2.5cm vegetable oil and bring to frying temperature (add a little bit of the batter: if it sizzles immediately, the oil is hot enough). Line a plate with a double layer of kitchen paper.

Meanwhile, peel and core the apples, then cut them into 5mm-thick slices.

Dip each apple slice in turn into the batter and shake off any excess, then carefully lower them into the hot oil and fry in batches, 5–6 slices at a time depending on the size of your pan, for about a minute on each side until the batter has puffed up and turned golden brown all over. Remove with a slotted spoon and transfer to the paper-lined plate to drain. While still hot, coat the fritters in the cinnamon sugar before serving.

Cinnamon Brioche Toast

The first time I tried Shibuya honey toast in Bangkok, I was completely smitten. Although it's very much a sweet treat of Japanese origin, there is much to love about a cube of buttered and sugared, pan-fried until crispy, pillowy white bread, smothered in more butter and drowned in honey with a scoop of vanilla ice cream on top. Although this quick and easy dessert/breakfast dish is inspired by Shibuya toast, it's much simpler and yet every bit as satisfying. If the cinnamon sugar exterior doesn't provide you with enough indulgence, a scoop of vanilla cream may just help seal the deal.

MAKES 4

3 tablespoons caster sugar

1 heaped teaspoon ground cinnamon, plus extra to decorate

60g butter, softened

4 slices of brioche loaf, about 2.5cm thick

For the vanilla cream (optional)

150ml double cream

1 teaspoon vanilla bean paste

If making the vanilla cream, whip the cream to soft peak stage, then stir in the vanilla paste. Set aside in the refrigerator while you cook the brioche toasts.

Mix the sugar and cinnamon together in a small bowl.

Heat a large frying pan over a medium heat (low-medium if using a gas hob).

Butter each slice of brioche on both sides. Take half the cinnamon sugar and sprinkle it on top of the 4 slices, patting it into the butter.

Once the pan is hot, add the brioche, sugar-side down. Add the remaining cinnamon sugar to the 4 slices, again patting it into the butter. Fry the slices for a couple of minutes on each side, checking that the sugar has caramelized on both sides.

Carefully remove the brioche slices from the pan to serving plates. Once the sugar cools, it will firm up on the brioche to form a lovely crunchy crust. Serve with the whipped vanilla cream sprinkled with extra ground cinnamon, if desired.

Feta, Basil & Strawberry Cheesecake Cups

I like to think of myself as a slightly whacky creator of desserts – nothing too complicated because I'm lazy, but now and again I like to put together something unusual that I know you will all enjoy. This is one such recipe . . . the feta element is inspired by my love for Honey & Co.'s feta and honey cheesecake. This is quite different, but I wanted to reference my lovely friends Sarit and Itamar because they are endlessly inspiring. I love combining fruit with herbs and this combination of flavours is a knockout. Don't believe me? Try it!

MAKES 4

50g unsalted butter, melted

8 digestive biscuits, crushed into crumbs

150g feta cheese, finely crumbled

250g full-fat cream cheese

100g caster sugar, plus 1 tablespoon

150ml double cream

½ packet (about 15g) of basil, leaves
   finely chopped, some reserved to decorate

400g strawberries, hulled

squeeze of lemon juice

Mix the melted butter with the crushed biscuit crumbs in a mixing bowl until evenly combined.

Crumble the feta into another mixing bowl, add the cream cheese and, using an electric hand whisk, beat together until as smooth as possible. Add the 100g sugar and whisk it in, then pour in the cream and add the chopped basil and whisk for a couple of minutes until evenly combined.

Blitz 100g of the strawberries with the tablespoon of sugar and lemon juice in a blender until liquidized. Finely dice the remaining strawberries and mix them into the strawberry mixture.

Divide the biscuit crumbs between 4 tumblers and press down to flatten and create biscuit crumb bases. Spoon an equal quantity of the cheesecake mixture over each crumb base, then top with an equal quantity of the strawberry mixture. Refrigerate for at least 2 hours or overnight before serving.

Lime, Coconut & Cardamom Loaf Cake

This is a wonderful combination of flavours and an excellent teatime treat. The sponge itself has the pleasing chewiness that I adore in cakes courtesy of the desiccated coconut, and the drizzle icing gives a lovely extra hit of coconut and lime for the finish. For a real afternoon delight, I love a slice with a nice cup of my favourite Yorkshire tea. The leftover coconut milk makes a fantastic addition to soups, curries and stews or even smoothies. Keep in the refrigerator and use within 24 hours, or freeze in ice-cube trays until needed.

SERVES 6–8

3 eggs

150g caster sugar

finely grated zest of 2 unwaxed limes, some reserved for decorating, and juice of 1

seeds from 6 green cardamom pods, ground using a pestle and mortar

1 teaspoon vanilla extract

50g desiccated coconut

400ml can coconut milk, solidified cream on top spooned off, leaving the liquid unused

150g plain flour

1 teaspoon baking powder

50g unsalted butter, melted

100g icing sugar, sifted, plus more if needed

handful of coconut flakes

Preheat the oven to 180°C (160°C fan), Gas Mark 4. Line a 2lb loaf tin with a nonstick paper liner, or cut a rectangle of baking paper, scrunch it up, then smooth it out and use to line the tin.

Put the eggs, caster sugar, lime zest and half the juice, the cardamom, vanilla, desiccated coconut and 3 level tablespoons of the coconut cream into a mixing bowl and use a wooden spoon to beat together until evenly combined. Add the flour, baking powder and melted butter and mix until smooth.

Pour the batter into the lined tin and bake for 1 hour, or until a skewer or knife inserted into the centre comes out clean. Remove from the oven and leave to cool in the tin.

Meanwhile, to make the icing, put the remaining coconut cream and lime juice into a bowl and beat in the icing sugar until smooth. Depending on the volume of lime juice, you may need to add a bit more icing sugar.

Turn out the cooled cake on to a wire rack. Spread the icing over the top, scatter with the reserved lime zest and coconut flakes, then leave to set and for the cake to cool completely. Cut into slices to serve.

Pistachio & Chocolate Dream Cake

This is the cake of my dreams, combining pistachios with chocolate in the most indulgent and spectacular way. There really is little I can add here because you will see what I mean when you make it.

SERVES 8

200g butter, softened, plus extra
   for greasing

200g caster sugar

1 teaspoon vanilla extract

4 large eggs

175g plain flour

2 teaspoons baking powder

200g pistachio slivers (or very roughly
   chopped whole nuts), very finely
   ground in a food processor

100ml milk

For the frosting

200g unsalted butter, softened

350g icing sugar

100g cocoa powder

1 heaped teaspoon vanilla bean paste

125ml double cream

pinch of Maldon sea salt flakes

Preheat the oven to 180°C (160°C fan), Gas Mark 4. Grease the sides of two 20cm sandwich tins with butter. Cut 2 discs of baking paper to fit the tin bases, then scrunch up and smooth out to line the bases.

Using an electric hand whisk, beat the butter, sugar and vanilla extract together in a large mixing bowl until light and fluffy. Then add the eggs and beat again until incorporated. Next, add the flour, baking powder and 100g of the ground pistachios and mix until smooth. Gradually pour in the milk and whisk in until completely incorporated and the batter is nice and loose.

Divide the batter between the prepared tins and bake for 30 minutes, or until a skewer inserted into the centre comes out clean. Remove from the oven, leave for 5 minutes, then turn out the cakes on to a wire rack, remove the baking paper and leave to cool.

To make the frosting, place all the ingredients in a large bowl and use an electric hand whisk or stand mixer to beat together until smooth. Spread a third of the frosting on top of one cake and scatter with one-third of the remaining ground pistachios. Sandwich the second cake on top and use the remaining frosting to coat the top and sides. Scatter over the remaining pistachios and serve. In warmer weather, you may wish to refrigerate the cake for an hour before serving.

Raspberry & Pistachio Crêpe Cake

I have chosen this particular combination as I simply adore pistachios with raspberries and, with the help of a little natural food colour, this little creation looks (and tastes) special indeed.

SERVES 6

100g plain flour, sifted

pinch of salt

2 eggs

200ml milk

50ml water

50g salted butter, melted, plus
    3 tablespoons, melted, for frying

1 heaped tablespoon golden caster
    sugar

For the filling

900ml double cream

6 tablespoons icing sugar

2 teaspoons vanilla bean paste

pink natural food colouring

75g pistachio slivers (or very roughly
    chopped whole nuts), very finely
    ground in a food processor

250g raspberries

To make the crêpe batter, put the flour, salt and eggs into a large mixing bowl. Mix the milk and water together in a jug, then whisk into the flour mixture a little at a time using either a fork or an electric hand whisk to beat out any lumps. Mix in the 50g melted butter and the caster sugar and set aside.

Heat a large frying pan over a medium-high heat. Drizzle in 1 teaspoon melted butter and tilt the pan to spread it around the base of the pan. Quickly pour in just enough crêpe batter to barely coat the base (you want a thin crêpe, not a pancake) and tilt the pan to spread the batter evenly to make a roughly 20cm crêpe. Cook for about 1 minute, or until the edges start to curl up and the underside is golden, then flip or turn the crêpe over with a spatula and cook for a further 30 seconds or so until golden brown on the other side. Transfer the crêpe to a plate and cover with a sheet of baking paper. Repeat with the remaining batter to make 8 crêpes in total, adding 1 teaspoon melted butter to the pan each time and stacking the cooked crêpes on the plate with baking paper in between each. Leave them to cool, then cover and keep cold in the refrigerator until ready to assemble the cake.

To make the filling, mix the cream with the icing sugar and vanilla bean paste in a large mixing bowl, then add some pink food colouring, a little at a time, until you reach the desired colour (some brands need more, some less). Using an electric hand whisk, whip the cream mixture until stiff, pillowy peaks form.

To assemble the cake, remove the crêpes from the refrigerator and place 1 on a serving plate, then spread with enough of the cream mixture to cover the surface. Repeat with the remaining crêpes until you have added the last one. Cover the top and exposed edges of the cake with the rest of the cream mixture, then scatter with the pistachios followed by the raspberries. Return the cake to the refrigerator for an hour to firm up before serving.

Sticky Coffee & Spice Cake

Sticky toffee pudding is among the nation's favourite puddings, and is a firm family favourite, too. There really is no messing with perfection, but this version, inspired by the aromatic cardamom-spiked coffees I drank endlessly in Dubai, is worth a try. The combination is just so good that I used it as a rich toffee-like sauce over a light, springy sponge, to make a lovely, more grown-up recipe that makes a warming, spiced dessert after an Eastern feast.

SERVES 9

For the cake

125g butter, softened, plus extra
    for greasing

3 eggs

200g light muscovado sugar

250g plain flour

1 teaspoon baking powder

1 teaspoon bicarbonate of soda

300ml milk

vanilla ice cream, to serve

For the coffee & spice sauce

seeds from 6 cardamom pods, finely
    ground using a pestle and mortar

½ teaspoon ground cinnamon

3 teaspoons coffee granules, dissolved
    in 2 tablespoons boiling water

150g light muscovado sugar

1 teaspoon vanilla bean paste

1 tablespoon black treacle

100g salted butter

300ml double cream

Preheat the oven to 180°C (160°C fan), Gas Mark 4. Grease a nonstick 20cm square cake tin with butter.

Put all the ingredients for the cake into a mixing bowl and beat together until well combined. Pour the batter into the greased tin and bake for 45 minutes, or until a skewer inserted into the centre comes out clean.

Meanwhile, stir all the sauce ingredients together in a saucepan and cook over a low heat until the sugar has dissolved and the sauce is smooth. Increase the heat and bring to a rolling boil for 1–2 minutes, then stir well and remove from the heat.

Remove the cake from the oven, then slice into squares and serve with the sauce poured over it and topped with a scoop of vanilla ice cream.

Tahini, Almond & Chocolate Crumble Cookies

I cannot tell you how satisfying these cookies are – so much so that I usually have a bag of the cookie dough balls stashed in my freezer ready for baking whenever the craving hits. The texture is crumbly in an almost sandy way and the absolute optimum moment to enjoy them is 30 minutes out of the oven, when the cookies have cooled down but the chocolate is still gooey. They are also great the next day provided you've stored them in an airtight container overnight, and are perfect for sharing with others . . . or not, if you're anything like me.

MAKES 14

125g salted butter, softened

125g soft light brown sugar

75g caster sugar

½ teaspoon ground cinnamon

100g tahini (use the solids and avoid the oil as much as possible)

150g plain flour

½ teaspoon baking powder

½ teaspoon bicarbonate of soda

50g blanched almonds, roughly chopped

200g dark chocolate chunks (70% cocoa solids)

Beat the softened butter, sugars and cinnamon together in a mixing bowl until light and fluffy. Then add the tahini and mix until smooth. Next, add the flour, baking powder and bicarbonate of soda and mix until evenly combined. Finally, add the almonds and dark chocolate chunks and mix until evenly distributed.

Weigh the cookie dough, divide into 14 equal portions and form each into a ball. Chill in the refrigerator for at least 4 hours, or overnight if preferred. Once chilled, you can then freeze the cookie dough balls for later use.

To bake, preheat the oven to 180°C (160°C fan), Gas Mark 4. Line a baking tray with baking paper.

Place your dough balls, well spaced out, on the lined tray and gently flatten them (omit this stage if using frozen dough). Bake for 16 minutes (or 18 from frozen). Remove from the oven and leave to cool on the tray for 30 minutes, then enjoy.

Tea, Cranberry, Orange & Macadamia Shortbreads

I have loved shortbread ever since I was a kid and I always thought it must be pretty difficult to make, but the best things in life (and food) usually tend to be very simple and happily shortbread proves to be no exception. It's also very versatile when it comes to flavour additions, with this particular combination being a standout winner for me, and these shortbreads really will make lovely gifts for deserving friends and loved ones. Although they keep well once baked, you can also halve the shortbread dough and freeze one-half for later use, then defrost and keep in the refrigerator until you're ready to bake.

MAKES 18–20

2 Earl Grey tea bags

300g plain flour

100g icing sugar

100g macadamia nuts or blanched almonds, roughly chopped

100g dried cranberries, roughly chopped

finely grated zest of 2 unwaxed oranges

1 teaspoon vanilla bean paste

pinch of salt

200g unsalted butter, softened

olive oil

caster sugar, for sprinkling

Split open the teabags and tip the tea into a large mixing bowl with the flour, icing sugar, nuts, cranberries, orange zest, vanilla and salt and mix together. Add the butter and just enough olive oil to work the mixture with your hands into an evenly combined ball of firm dough.

Roll the dough into a log about 4–5cm in diameter. Wrap tightly in clingfilm and twist the ends to encase the dough tightly, like a sweet wrapper. Chill in the refrigerator for at least an hour or overnight.

Preheat the oven to 150°C (130°C fan), Gas Mark 2. Line a large baking tray with baking paper.

Unwrap the dough, cut into 1cm-thick discs and place on the lined tray, about 2cm apart, then sprinkle liberally with caster sugar. Bake for 20 minutes, or until the edges turn slightly golden.

Remove from the oven and leave to cool on the tray, which allows the shortbreads to firm up. Once completely cool, they are ready to enjoy.

Index